Inventory

One stone
two houses
three ruins
four grave-diggers
one garden
some flowers

one racoon

a dozen oysters a lemon a loaf of bread
a ray of sunlight
one groundswell
six musicians
one door with doormat
one Mister decorated with the Legion of Honour

one more racoon

one sculptor who sculpts Napoleons
one yellow flower called care
two lovers on a big bed
one receiver of contributions one chair three turkeys
one cleric one boil
one wasp
one floating kidney
one racing stable
one unworthy son two Dominican brothers three
    grasshoppers one collapsible chair
two whores one amorous uncle
one *mater dolorosa* three sugar daddies two goats belonging
    to Mister Seguin
one Louis the Fifteenth heel
one Louis the Sixteenth armchair
one Henry the Second sideboard two Henry the Third
    sideboards three Henry the Fourth sideboards

THE PARIS FLEA MARKET

LES PUCES DE PARIS, SAINT-OUEN

KATE VAN DEN BOOGERT
WITH PHOTOGRAPHY BY TOBY GLANVILLE

PRESTEL
MUNICH · LONDON · NEW YORK

© Prestel Verlag,
Munich · London · New York, 2024
A member of Penguin Random House Verlagsgruppe GmbH
Neumarkter Strasse 28 · 81673 Munich

© for the texts by Kate van den Boogert, 2024
© for the works of art by Toby Glanville, 2024

Cover: Don Shoemaker for Señal S.A., solid rosewood chair,
circa 1960, see p. 102
Back cover: A 20th-century copy of the head of Michelangelo's *David*
from Bernard Tinivella's stand at the Marché Paul Bert, see p. 122

Library of Congress Control Number is available; a CIP catalogue
record for this book is available from the British Library.

Editorial direction: Rochelle Roberts
Translation: Kate van den Boogert
Copyediting: Francine Brody
Graphic design: Change is Good, Rik Bas Backer & José Albergaria
Production management: Corinna Pickart
Separations: Schnieber Graphik GmbH, Munich
Printing and binding: TBB, a.s., Banská Bystrica
Typefaces: Flea Market; Mabry
Paper: Magno Natural

Penguin Random House Verlagsgruppe FSC® N001967

Printed in Slovakia

ISBN 978-3-7913-7973-9

www.prestel.com

CONTENTS

14   Introduction by Kate van den Boogert

20   ALBERT & ROXANE RODRIGUEZ

Marché Jules Vallès

32   SAMUEL COLLIN

Marché Paul Bert

44   VALÉRIE BOUVIER & ANTOINE NOUVET

56   PHILIPPE STARCK 'Why We Love the Puces'

58   FRANÇOIS-XAVIER COURRÈGES

70   MAXIME DE LAURENTIS

82   NATHALIE DUPUIS

94   KARL FOURNIER & OLIVIER MARTY 'Why We Love the Puces'

96   MAX KEYS

108   EVA STEINITZ

120   BERNARD TINIVELLA

132   BENOÎT ASTIER DE VILLATTE & IVAN PERICOLI 'Why We Love the Puces'

134   LAURENCE VAUCLAIR & DENIS ROUQUETTE

Marché Serpette

146   HUGO GREINER

158   AURÉLIEN SERRE

170   RAMDANE TOUHAMI 'Why We Love the Puces'

Marché Dauphine

172   FRANÇOISE & ERWAN DE FLIGUÉ

184   JEAN-PAUL JURQUET

Marché Vernaison

196   DOMINIQUE JAMES

208   JACQUES GARCIA 'Why We Love the Puces'

210   CHARLES MAS

222   DAMIEN VANNIENWENHOVE

Marché Biron

234   JEAN-LUC FERRAND

247   A Chronology of Antique French Furniture Periods

INTRO-
DUCTION

Stretching out over almost five acres at the northern gates of Paris, just beyond the *boulevard périphérique*, or ring road, lies the world's most epic antiques, collectibles and junk market. A wild and sprawling city within a city, strange and enchanted, the Puces de Paris Saint-Ouen flea market is without equivalent in the world.

This book draws back the curtain on the much-talked-about but actually quite secret and impenetrable world of the Puces, presenting a sample of the dealers at its heart. Bright constellations in a crowded galaxy, each one an avatar of a particular expertise, they show us memorable finds and conjure private voodoo. They introduce us to artisans and other essential collaborators, share personal Paris landmarks, let us in on trade secrets. This book gives you a chance to look closely at this cluster of stars as if through a telescope, leaning in and focusing until everything begins to gleam.

The Puces, taken as a whole, requires you to correct your vision; to adjust eyes that have been trained by the twenty-first century, in the tidy shops, malls, catalogues and e-shops of the West, loaded with their perfect industrially made products, uniform and predictable, available in every size and colour. The Puces asks you to upturn typical shopping habits, to favour instinct over advertising, personality over perfection, eccentricity over good taste, mystery over rationality, one-off and hand-made over factory-made, yesterday over tomorrow, mess over order, and poetry over business.

Vincent van Gogh, *Outskirts of Paris, View from Montmartre*, 1887.

This curious and crazy place evolved out of a unique conjunction of circumstances – geographical, cultural, and political – catalysed by Baron Eugene von Haussmann's radical modernization of Paris that began in 1853. The disparate bunch of dealers there today, like those at the other Paris flea markets of Montreuil and Vanves, descend from a community of *chiffonniers*, or ragpickers. Along with many other 'undesirables' – migrants, Gypsies, Jews, the poor – they began to settle in a borderland in between Paris and its surrounding suburbs known as *la Zone*. This 250-metre-wide, non-constructible military belt ran alongside the Thiers wall, Paris's last set of fortifications completed in 1844, and became a kind of shanty town ringing the capital.

The Thiers wall, the ditch, the defensive embankment, and children from *la Zone* grazing their goats, 1913.

Chiffonniers, or *biffins*, as they're known in the local Parisian argot, were firmly entrenched in the daily life of Paris by then. Pliers of an ancient profession, for centuries they played a vital part in the removal and recycling of the city's waste. Each night, many thousands of them sifted through what was left out for the streetsweepers, recuperating not just the *chiffons*, or rags, which were reused to make paper, but many other interesting and useful scraps too. La Vargouleme, a *chiffonnier* in Victor Hugo's 1862 novel *Les Misérables* describes how he handled his haul: 'In the morning, on my return home, I pick over my basket, I sort my things. This makes heaps in my room. I put the rags in a basket, the cores and stalks in a bucket, the linen in my cupboard, the woollen stuff in my commode, the old papers in the corner of the window, the things that are good to eat in my bowl, the bits of glass in my fireplace, the old shoes behind my door, and the bones under my bed.'

View of *la Zone* near Porte de Clignancourt, with the city of Saint-Ouen in the background, c. 1940.

Near the bottom of the social order with drunks, beggars and prostitutes, and with a well-earned reputation for proud and savage independence, the *chiffonniers* both fascinated and repulsed polite society. Artists and writers, from Baudelaire to Manet, were inspired by their outsider vagabond status, and even identified with it. Photographers like Eugène Atget and Germaine Krull brought them out of the shadows, into the light.

Lying just to the north of *la Zone* and its community of ragpickers was the village of Saint-Ouen, like so many other riverside villages ringing Paris, a destination much loved by Sunday strollers. On their day off, working-class Parisians might wander up from Montmartre, through the Porte de Clignancourt, stopping perhaps on the grassy ramparts of the *fortifs*, before continuing on to Saint-Ouen to enjoy its bars and *guinguettes* serving a cheap local white, or to try their luck at its racecourse, which was built in 1880.

This Sunday exodus — which you can see celebrated in the work of artists including Monet, Caillebotte, Van Gogh, Seurat or Renoir — provided a steady clientele for the *chiffonniers*. Alongside them there emerged *brocanteurs,* more specialized second-hand traders with their own sources and methods. Though after 1883, both would have to contend with the new-fangled rubbish bin, imposed by town prefect Eugène Poubelle, which complicated their businesses. (*Poubelle* is still the word used for rubbish bin in French today.)

Georges Seurat, *Bathers at Asnières*, 1884.

As the city organized its disposal rules, the Puces took shape to provide an officially sanctioned selling ground. From 1891, a fee was demanded from those who unpacked their finds along the pavement of the Avenue Michelet on Sunday. Around the same time, the area started to develop and upscale: the Metro came to the Porte de Clignancourt in 1908, the streets of Saint-Ouen were paved, and the fortifications that divided the village from the city centre were demolished in 1919.

After the First World War, the trade in second-hand goods began to specialize, and collectors followed in its wake. Businesses grew to meet demand, and entrepreneurs bought up land to equip it with simple stalls they rented out to merchants. Romain Vernaison, a concessionaire at Les Halles food market, who also rented chairs in Parisian public gardens, installed prefabricated wooden huts on land he owned in Saint-Ouen — some of them are still standing — and the Puces' first properly structured market opened in 1920. It still bears his name today.

A summer picnic in Saint-Ouen, postcard, c. 1910.

The Puces, with its incongruous profusion and juxtapositions, at the intersection of the primitive and the sophisticated, of dreams and waking reality, was a lodestar for the Surrealists. Artists like Alberto Giacometti and André Breton found a fecund site for the *hasard objectif*, or objective chance encounter, as well as the *objet trouvé*, or found object. For them, the synchronicities that were so easily occasioned at the Puces catalysed thoughts and desires, and let the unconscious speak. 'I go there often, searching for objects that can be found nowhere else: old-fashioned, broken, useless, almost incomprehensible, even perverse,' Breton wrote in his 1928 novel *Nadja*. Later, after the war, the writer Jacques Prévert, poet of the people and a friend to the Surrealists, created collages from images he found at the Puces. And his poem 'Inventaire', a mad and joyous list of seemingly random impressions, could describe a typical day there. (Skip to this book's endpapers to read a fragment of it, alongside its 1958 English translation by Lawrence Ferlinghetti.)

Poubelles on the footpath, Rue Emile Zola, Paris, 1913.

Shopping the Puces today takes you through eleven different markets that function like a collection of tiny neighbourhoods, each with its own history and identity. Having grown organically, not through planning, the different spaces make for a motley compendium of styles and structures. It's like a delightful favela with very little architectural harmony, modern comfort or conventional beauty, whose eccentricity only adds to its charm.

Every one of the individual markets has its own niche and speciality. Marché Vernaison, the original, looks like what you'd imagine when you hear the words 'flea market': a picturesque tangle of alleyways lined with about 250 rickety little stands selling all sorts of bric-à-brac. Stretching over practically 9,000 square metres, it's the biggest market in the Puces.

Opposite Vernaison, the two-storey, glass-roofed Marché Dauphine opened in 1991 and presents a mix of pop-culture ephemera – records, posters, postcards, books, comics – vintage fashion and accessories, and quality antiques. The Marché Biron, which dates back to 1925, ups the bling factor with a red carpet along its long central avenue, as if it were Cannes during festival time. Biron was the first to sell restored old objects and today specializes in high-end '*antiquités classiques*', meaning pre-Modern, pre-twentieth-century pieces.

There's been a major cultural shift at the Puces over the past couple of decades, as twentieth-century furniture overtakes *classique*, for so long the lifeblood here. Today, the Marché Paul Bert and the adjacent Marché Serpette – a former car park converted in the 70s – both specializing in twentieth-century goods, are the Puces' most design-forward and high-profile markets.

The long, covered Marché Jules Vallès opened in 1938 and is reputed for having good deals and a rapid turnover of unrestored pieces, attracting many dealers. The Marché L'Usine next door is also more business-to-business, open in principle to professionals only, on weekdays, when the rest of the market is closed. A handful of other, smaller markets complete the picture, including the Marché Malik with its fake Balenciaga and Jacquemus, Nikes or Ray-Bans.

The Puces has always been home to an important number of Jewish dealers, dating back to a first wave of immigration from Russia in the late 1800s. With a cultural history tied to tailoring and clothing repair, many of these immigrants were tailors, hat makers, or dealers in second-hand clothing who found a natural home here. The Marché Paul Bert, created in 1946 on the site of an old vineyard, offered a percentage of its stands to Jewish dealers, which allowed them to resume trade after the devastation and horror of the Second World War.

If the trade at a few of the established markets at the Puces is today exceptionally noble and refined, five market streets – Rue Jules Vallès, Rue Lecuyer, Rue Paul Bert, Rue des Rosiers and Impasse Simon – are home to a mix of makeshift stands, shops, and pavement sellers continuing the trade of the *biffins*. Everything imaginable that can be sold or collected is found here. Old valves. Sweat socks. Spent ammunition shells. Shoelaces. Doll's heads. Why not? Everybody's trash is somebody's treasure.

From the most hallowed expert and cashed-up collector to the humblest street seller, everyone finds sustenance and joy at a large array of cafés and restaurants scattered throughout the Puces or close by. There are charming traditional bistros, couscous joints, down and dirty dives, the jazz manouche mecca La Chope des Puces, even two separate MOB boutique hotels, with their garden terraces and excellent pizza. Almost all of it has survived Covid, with the sad exception of Chez Louisette, the historic music hall and *guinguette* once located inside Vernaison market. (All that remains of it now are video clips of its warbling torch singers and day-drunk crowds that haunt the internet like ghosts of the dearly departed.)

A bronze cast, c. 1900, of a glove fetishized by the narrator in André Breton's *Nadja*; an iconic 'surrealist object', the sculpture was lent to Breton by Lise Deharme to illustrate the novel.

Chez Louisette, c. 1950.

Open on the weekends and partly on Mondays too, the Puces draws crowds of tourists and locals who come to wander the alleys, hang out, and *chiner*. A concept so specifically French it's essentially untranslatable, *chiner* means to meander, more or less aimlessly, while perusing old stuff. You can't *chiner* new things. It's not quite antiquing, bargain hunting or digging. It describes a state of browsing without knowing what you're looking for, a journey more than a destination. Like that other untranslatable French word *flâner*, which was invented to describe a new, modern relationship to the urban spectacle, *chiner* is almost a state of mind, a philosophy of life. It's the religion of the Puces. It's the art and *raison d'être* of the dealers.

You can *chiner* your way through the entire country, as every city, town and neighbourhood throughout France is proud host to regular *brocantes* and *vide-greniers,* or garage sales. This French way of life is visible too in the Puces' colourful demonstration of the Socialist principle of *'mixité',* or social diversity. Perhaps it's no coincidence that Saint-Ouen, where the Puces was born and thrived, is emblematic of the 'red belt' of northeastern suburbs. Between 1945 and 2014, Saint-Ouen had just three mayors, all Communist. Is this what allowed the market to resist the pressures of big business and the property market? At London's Portobello Market, rising rents and an absence of regulation have seen a once glorious heap of treasures overrun by chains selling new goods, largely tat for tourists. The number of antique dealers there has more than halved since the 90s.

John Gay, *Portobello Road Market*, London, 1962.

Aside from politics, it's that blurry poetic thing called 'atmosphere' that protects the Puces from the threat of gentrification today. After one fifth of the overall market was lost to property development, in 2001 the Puces was designated a Zone for the Protection of Architectural, Urban, and Landscape Heritage. This status safeguards from destruction or significant modification, and formally recognizes the Puces as a site of intangible heritage, more than the sum of its parts. An application underway for UNESCO World Heritage status should provide even stronger protection, at an international level.

The Puces' countless dealers – is it one thousand or two? No one seems able to say with any certainty – each participate in their own way in a sinuous human network that empties the houses and apartments of France and Europe, the crumbling châteaux, old shops and factories, safety deposit boxes. Everything humanity has produced, the ill-gotten gains and splendid inheritances, just keep piling up, and the dealers today, like the *chiffonniers* of the nineteenth century, sift and sort through the mountains of possessions that have been forgotten, lost, reclaimed, confiscated, overlooked, given up, or sacrificed in our collective march through time. All this drains into the Puces like an estuary into the sea.

Typically, each dealer sells what they love most, sharing their passions fully. Each stand is an altar to someone's unique taste, expertise and obsessions. Few consult trend reports about next season's favourite colour or conduct keyword searches. Instead, the Puces is a jumble of idiosyncrasy and self-expression. If some dealers have degrees in art history, auctioneering or business, most of them have more improvised CVs. There's no real school for what they do. Many of the dealers you will meet in these pages continue a family heritage, others fell into the business from individual passion or a chance encounter. The market's rich character is the collective expression of these largely unconventional lives.

New trends certainly do emerge out of the Puces, though, and each dealer's taste, expertise and flair contributes, making the old new again, reinvigorating the market with forgotten talents and styles, and teaching wide-eyed *chineurs* to see differently. Furniture designed by Jean Prouvé and other Modernist architects was worth peanuts before being rediscovered in the 80s by dealers at the Puces. In creating a market for things that used not to have one, dealers reconfigure the landscape of supply and demand. Sometimes it comes from opportunism, seeing the profit in things that are easy and affordable to source, and sometimes through the force of their conviction, and their trailblazing taste.

Another crucial strand of DNA making up the Puces is its flourishing community of highly skilled artisans, many of them working in the old way, out of workshops hidden amongst the market's streets and alleys. The Puces valorises and maintains artisanal skills that have, in many other cities in the world, almost disappeared. Cabinetmakers, gilders, art restorers, chandelier repairers, ceramic restorers, marble workers, electricians, upholsterers, glassmakers, metalsmiths, and more, give new life and lustre to objects that have already survived decades or centuries.

This open-air museum is a mecca not just for the *flâneur*, *chineur* or collector, but also for creative professionals, some of whom you will meet in this book. Decorators, architects, fashion and costume designers, furniture and set designers, artists and artisans of all sorts come to research, source, and buy, now more than ever preferring to recycle, upcycle and restore treasures from the past, rather than continuing to thoughtlessly over-produce.

Visiting the Puces is to land in the middle of an extraordinary catalogue of mankind's sensibility and imagination. It's a time machine passing through the history of civilizations, from Ancient Rome to Art Deco, the Middle Ages to Mid-Century Modern, the Renaissance to Memphis Milano, faster and with more fun than Google. A tribute to human endeavour, ingenuity, and love of beauty, it is a privilege to wander its alleys, to be able to soak it up #IRL, to see and touch the objects, sense their vibrations, and observe and mix with this rare human tapestry. The Puces demands new forms of interaction with the environment. With its variety and profusion, it's an invitation to sharpen your eye. And learning to 'see' is an adventure that gets more and more captivating the further you go. The best part of it is, entry is free.

Antiques and decoration;
the Puces de Saint Ouen's biggest
warehouse

ALBERT & ROXANE RODRIGUEZ

What is your expertise, speciality or particularity?
A: I am a generalist. We sell essentially nineteenth century, but we also have eighteenth- and seventeenth-century objects from time to time, Art Nouveau, Art Deco … a bit of everything.

Why the Puces?
A: There will always be objets d'art. Once man satisfies his primary needs: to eat, drink and sleep, and when he has the means, he wants to give himself an intellectual dimension, so he buys objets d'art, and creates a unique environment for himself that differentiates him from, and impresses, others. This has always existed in all civilizations.

Tell us about your profession.
A: Objets d'art are a matter of sensitivity, and each dealer is attracted by different objects. Basically, it's personal taste. Then there are fashions that many follow, but I'm from the old guard, and currently the trend in the market is more twentieth century. It's a little surprising, because they're not exactly antiques, given the very short time frame, but it's the same business as ours.

How did you get where you are?
A: I started on a moped, because in 1971 I didn't have my driver's license yet. I wanted to make some pocket money, I was still in high school. I was selling a lot of cameras, then I came to objets d'art because the mother of one of my friends was a collector, and we started looking for small pieces for her; we went to Drouot and all those places. And as I got married very young, I had to support my family. The early seventies was a favourable time. When they demolished the Front de Seine in the 15th arrondissement, all the buildings were expropriated. We distributed leaflets to the concierges and cleared apartments, then went to sell at the Montreuil flea market. And then I came to Saint Ouen; I started selling on the sidewalk, then I had a stand in Jules Vallès, then Serpette, then Rue Lecuyer, then L'Usine, and so on.

You wouldn't be where you are without …?
R: I am a child of the Puces. My mother, Marianne, who passed away in 2012, was a figure at the Puces, just as much as Papa. She was a very vibrant and luminous person, and very well liked. She had a passion for her profession. Most antique dealers work in tandem in a small business where the husband goes hunting, and the wife takes care of sales and accounting. That's how my parents started.

What has, or hasn't, changed at the Puces?
A: With the pressure from property developers, 20 per cent of the Puces has disappeared. The price of land at the gates of Paris arouses the interest of developers, and that's the main threat. In 1995 with Marc Maison, we founded an association to defend the interests of the Puces. The city lost three successive court cases, and we managed to get the Puces classified as a Zone for Protection of Architectural, Urban and Landscape heritage (ZPPAUP), which is a solid form of protection. When I was president of the association, there were two things that concerned me: generational renewal – I thought of creating a school, to preserve the know-how, and create an elite group of dealers; and the UNESCO classification, which is currently underway, and will provide far greater protection for the Puces.

How does the Puces relate to the larger antiques and second-hand market in Paris, and around the world?
A: It's always the dealers who create the trends. My daughter Roxane, for example, is a decorator, and it was she who, along with Roberto Polo, made nineteenth-century designers fashionable. Fashions are the passion of mankind, and evolve constantly, are constantly changing. It's always fashion that creates the market.

Does research and documentation take up a lot of your time?
R: When Papa brings in pieces that I find interesting, I love researching them, it's a passion. It's like being a detective, and you get satisfaction for yourself, but also for the artist. Also, in the act of delving deeper, infinite connections are made between the world of the dead and that of the living. The history of the object of yesterday and today is intrinsically linked to the history of man. Through research, we learn from our collective unconscious.

Your favourite period, movement, or style?
A: The Régence period is quite short, about twenty years, and saw the evolution from Louis XIV style towards Louis XV style. Louis XIV style evolved from the renaissance period, when the furniture was a little rustic, a little heavy, and after Louis XV it is very sugary. Regency is between the two, it's the beginning of refinement without having the mannerism, the schmaltziness of Louis XIV. It's a beautiful period when great cabinetmakers made very beautiful furniture.

Essential artisan or craft for you?
A: For three centuries from Louis XIV, there was a concentration of craftsmanship in the Faubourg Saint-Antoine quarter in Paris. All the skills were assembled in the same place – now we call it a cluster – which created a dynamic. I don't have the statistics, but at the end of the nineteenth, beginning of the twentieth, there were maybe over a thousand artisans – gilders, cabinetmakers, marquetry workers – working there for the decorative arts, but now I'm not sure there are even ten left.

A good anecdote?
A: This is a true story. Two chairs arrived at the Puces a couple of years ago. A dealer from Paul Bert found them in the street, he only sold paintings, but he picked them up because he thought they were beautiful, they deserved to be saved. The seats smelled of damp, they stank on his stand, so he asked a dealer in Jules Vallès if he could sell the chairs, and they would split the price. So he took them; a customer comes by, haggles the price down from 1,000 to 800 euros, but by half past twelve still hasn't paid. The guy is fed up, another customer comes by, 'How much do you want for the armchairs', '1,000 euros' 'Ok'. He took them right away, boom, boom, boom. The armchairs were by Jean-Michel Frank. They ended up in a gallery Rue de Seine, with a 100,000-euro price tag. That's what's called hitting the jackpot.

Japonisme – 'This is a rather exceptional cabinet, c. 1880, by Gabriel Viardot, in mahogany and Japanese lacquer, belonging to the Japonisme movement. Following the opening of Japan to the West around 1860, there was a craze for all things Japanese. French cabinetmakers like Viardot and Édouard Lièvre took a close interest in Japanese craft and technique, and produced furniture inspired by Japan. This piece is rather exceptional because it is very probable that the lacquers were made in Japan. The most beautiful lacquers in the world are Japanese, there is a technical perfection there that has never been attained in Europe.'

The Ancient World – 'I started collecting Tanagra figurines about ten years ago. Tanagras are small figurines found in ancient Greek tombs. One of the houses that I dream of the most is the Villa Kerylos in Beaulieu-sur-Mer, commissioned at the start of the twentieth century by the great archaeologist Théodore Reinach from the architect Emmanuel Pontremoli. Built according to the Greek tradition of the second and first century BC, the villa is filled with ancient Greek artefacts. I know that my passion for Tanagras comes from the beauty and tranquillity of this place.'

The Strange Life of Objects — 'Collecting can be compulsive, or on the contrary, very specific. The first motivation is the desire for the "object" that we don't have, and which can cause frustration by its absence. Maurice Rheims in *The Strange Life of Objects* describes this perfectly — he devotes an entire chapter to the psychology of the collector.'

Trade Secret – 'Nicolas is with me three days a week. In general we completely rewire chandeliers so that they meet contemporary safety standards – so that there's not a fire at the customer's after we sell him a chandelier! It takes about 7–10 days per chandelier. We have a big stock of parts, of the crystal droplets. There's no equivalent quality in new pieces, especially for anything engraved. Chandeliers represent 5–10 per cent of my annual turnover. Sometimes we rent them for cinema and events; for example, we rented twenty to Louis Vuitton for a fashion show back in 2021.'

2240 — 1903.

Origin Story – Eugène Atget, *View of Palace and Sculpture, Versailles, France*, c. 1900. 'France dominated the decorative arts for two centuries; we were the absolute reference throughout the world, since Louis XIV, and because of Versailles. The construction of Versailles developed the decorative arts and craftsmanship in an extremely significant way. The best craftsmen in Europe came to France, and it created a melting pot, and an exchange of ideas that created fashions. Everyone wanted to copy the King. Even other European courts and the Russian court were furnished by the French, the French cabinetmakers of the Faubourg Saint-Antoine.'

The Secret Life of the Puces — 'I work with many different craftspeople, such as the gilder Isabelle Autour, who has her atelier Autour de l'Or here in the Puces, and restores the gilding on pieces like frames, mirrors, and many consoles for me. At one time I had a workshop with three employees, but now I subcontract.'

Street Furniture – 'A very beautiful monumental cast-iron fountain composed of a base decorated with shells and water lily leaves. The gadrooned basin, surrounded by water lily flowers, supports three cherubs in the Italian style of Renaissance "putti", placed around a generous bouquet of reeds. The Val d'Osne foundry was a French ornamental foundry. I think it's one of the most beautiful foundries in the world. Created in 1835 by Jean-Pierre-Victor André to manufacture street furniture and decorative cast iron, the factory quickly became the largest production site of ornamental cast iron in France. There are many large fountains like this one adorning town squares throughout France.'

Albert & Roxane Rodriguez

30

For Sale – Henry Dasson desk. Precious wood veneer, finely chiselled and gilded bronze, leather. Stamped and dated 1882. 'This desk is a copy of a Louis XV desk. At the end of the nineteenth century, the French bourgeoisie was very rich, and cabinetmakers started copying large pieces of eighteenth-century French furniture, often plagiarising royal furniture, that of Louis XV or Louis XVI for instance, but with a technical perfection and virtuosity made possible by the nascent mechanization of the industry. Henry Dasson was a great cabinetmaker, and his was a great Parisian workshop during the era of Napoleon III. In general, the furniture that came out of Dasson's ateliers was 99 per cent perfect.'

SAMUEL
COLLIN

What is your expertise, speciality or particularity?
Folk art and traditions, specifically pre-twentieth-century folk pottery (terrines, surname jugs, anthropomorphic roof finials, glazed kitchen water fountains …); unusual pieces by craftsmen and master craftsmen; wrought iron (keys, locks, andirons, pothooks …); carved wooden objects (pieces from Queyras, Breton wedding spoons, Norman and other wedding chests, snuff boxes, hunting mugs …); old glassware (eighteenth-century, Norman …); art brut, and dissident objects by convicts, sailors …; Haute Epoque (Middle Ages, the Renaissance and the early Baroque age).

Did you choose your market at the Puces?
Yes, absolutely, the Jules Vallès market is an authentic market, where the dealers source from 'adresses', that is, from private individuals. In the business, there are different ways of working, there are different ways to source goods, but everything comes from people's homes to begin with, and in Jules Vallès, a lot of the dealers buy directly from individuals. Whereas at Paul Bert, Serpette markets etc., most of the dealers buy from other dealers. We always say that the difference between a *brocanteur,* a second-hand dealer, and an antique dealer is that the second-hand dealer is the one who buys from individuals, who buys anything and everything, who is not necessarily a specialist in anything, though he may have affinities. He's the wholesaler to other dealers, because he doesn't necessarily have the customer for everything he buys, so he must sell through intermediaries. The antique dealer is more specialized. The merchants who are specialized buy from other dealers or in auctions, and also a lot from professional markets. I do both. For example, I might end up buying a bronze clock, but I don't have the customer for a bronze clock, and it's not necessarily something that interests me either, so I will sell it to a colleague, who has a buyer for it. Today with my folk art, I buy about 80 per cent from other dealers, I pay a little more, but I can choose the merchandise, that corresponds to my customers, and to what I like, it's already preselected, which saves time.

Who is your hero?
Leonidas I. I was interested in history from a very young age, from primary school. Some of the first books I read were Homer's the *Iliad* and the *Odyssey*, in children's editions, and from then I became interested in history, and at different times have been fascinated by the Middle Ages, antiquity … I was very interested in the American Indians, the American Civil War …

A favourite film?
Braveheart (1995). One aspect of history that interests me is Scotland's first wars of independence – Sir William Wallace who fought for the independence of Scotland and Robert the Bruce, who became King of Scotland.

I have a time machine; where do we go?
The Battle of Hastings, 14 October 1066. It's the Norman in me. These wars between France and England started a cycle that ended in 1815 in Waterloo. William the Conqueror changed the world. The Duchy of Normandy was a very powerful state in the tenth to eleventh centuries, enormously influential, and at the origin of the feudal systems of the Roman and Gothic eras. Most people are not that interested, it gets played down.

An unforgettable piece or sale?
A Viking sword, that dates from 900 and something. It was my dream to have one and it broke my heart at the time that I couldn't afford to buy it myself. In this business, there are times when you have money, then times when you don't have any money at all. The gentleman who owned it had inherited it from his father, who had found it in the Seine close to Rouen, near the Île des Oiseaux, a site of early Viking settlements. He and his friends discovered a drakkar in fact, and divvied up everything they found among them. I could only afford a spearhead. After the Second World War, all the rivers of France were full of junk – for centuries people had thrown stuff into the rivers, and after the war, there were actual plane wrecks, tanks. So from 1945 to 1947, there was a national effort to dredge the rivers. And at the time, the archaeological services did not exist like they do today, so if someone made an interesting discovery he could keep it. These are the conditions in which this sword was discovered.

A regret?
That the Musée National des Arts et Traditions Populaires in the Bois de Boulogne closed. It was a very interesting museum, the place in Paris that interested me the most. Many people like me deplored its closing, there were petitions. Someone said the problem with 'popular arts and traditions' is that the term 'popular' doesn't appeal to the Right, and the term 'tradition' doesn't appeal to the Left, which might explain why this museum disappeared. There are folk art museums in many regions in France: Normandy, Alsace, Brittany, but it's a pity that in the capital, this museum, which was extraordinary, was abolished.

Where does your inspiration come from?
From my father who used to scavenge through what was thrown on the street, and found beautiful objects … arousing my curiosity. There were no recycling centres like there are today, people put everything they had to throw away in the street, and before the garbage trucks passed, people whose job it was, *chiffonniers* or ragpickers, went through everything, and they're who originally sold to the Puces, to flea markets. Now it's gentrified we could say, but the origin of the Puces was that. It was people who scavenged in Paris and around, and then went to sell what they had collected at night or in the early morning. My father didn't do this for commercial purposes, because he resold practically nothing, but he collected for himself, for us, for the family, everything good he found, and he found really extraordinary things.

Samuel Collin

For Sale – 'This glass jug decorated with spiralling threads dates from the eighteenth century and was produced in a glassworks in the Orne region in Lower Normandy. Prior to the French Revolution, glass blowing was really considered a noble art, so was the privilege of the nobility. And it's interesting to know that wine was produced almost everywhere in France, even in Normandy, until around 1900 and the phylloxera epidemic. Normandy only turned to cider after the grape vines were uprooted.'

For Sale – 'This is a carved peasant scene in walnut, with eyes inlaid in bone, dating from the late nineteenth century and characteristic of what artisans were doing at that time. This is perhaps Dutch or German, judging by the style of the headdress of the woman milking the cow. The woman with the violin on her back is a beggar, asking for a bowl of milk. I'm not only interested in France; folk art exists all over Europe and the world.'

Samuel Collin

Private Property – 'This horn snuff box is engraved *Jean Piver Garde 1825* on the back, it must have belonged to a game warden. In 1825 in France we were in the midst of the Bourbon Restoration, there are fleur-de-lis on it, so he must have been a royalist. We see all the attributes of a hunter – a rifle and a pickaxe are crossed over a hunting horn, and there's a hunting scene on the lid. A hunter is holding his rifle, with his dog, aiming at birds in a naive leafy setting. It is a rare piece, a typical folk-art object that is particularly interesting because it is both dated and signed by its owner.'

Best Find – 'In 1993 or 1994, I participated in a professional sale of part of a large estate, the abbaye du Breuil-Benoît, which had belonged to the Comte de Reiset, who was an important collector at the end of the nineteenth century. At the sale, I found, in a shoebox, amongst postcards and all sorts of things of no great interest, a daguerreotype, under glass, which depicted a funeral in front of Notre-Dame, and written on the back was, "Burial of Monsignor the Duke of Orleans, which I attended, it is a great loss for France, July 30, 1842". I knew nothing at all about daguerreotypes or photography in general, but I understood immediately that it was a historical event, a page from the history of France, so I put it aside, but I couldn't find anyone at the time to sell it to. It was only a few years later that I met an expert in photography and when I showed him, he said "Indeed it is very, very interesting," and he identified the photographer. It went to auction in 1996, and the Musée d'Orsay bought it. It was the first photograph to sell for a high price, a record that has been largely exceeded since. It made headlines again recently, after the fire at Notre-Dame. Apparently it's the only known photograph of Notre-Dame before Viollet-le-Duc added the spire.'

Sentimental Value – 'I have been passionate about everything medieval, Viking, and Celt since I was a kid, so my father made me this sword to surprise me when I was about 13. Since it was his profession, he knew how to forge, to lathe. I don't think there are many people today who own a sword that was forged especially for them.'

Samuel Collin

Special Interest – 'A painted Rouen chest, early nineteenth century. The light blue background bordered in white, decorated with flowers and birds, in particular the stylized acanthus leaves, tulips and narcissus, is typical of the Aubry factory and of this period. These wooden chests were made practically only in Rouen. I always have some on my stand as they are one of my specialities. I even participated in an exhibition dedicated to the subject at the Château de Martainville, a museum of Norman folk art and traditions, in 2019. The production of these chests began in the middle of the eighteenth century and lasted until the 1870s, they must have been quite fashionable at the time. They were made from beech wood, though some later ones were made of pine, and always painted. They were commonly found in dowries, and the largest were used as travel trunks.'

Folk Pottery – 'Brissard is a hamlet in the Eure Valley in Normandy where an important pottery was in activity for at least a hundred years, from the late eighteenth century. Brissard pottery is of good quality, rather solid, because it was intended for daily use in rural areas. These demijohns dating from the nineteenth century are typical of Brissard pottery, and were intended for any type of beverage: water, cider, wine ... The typical green glaze is the result of the use of copper oxide. Folk pottery is really what I know best, it's my area of specialization.'

Liberté, égalité, fraternité – 'This is an allegory of the French Republic, carved in wood. The four figures in the picture are a blacksmith representing craftsmanship, a woman with a scythe representing agriculture, a soldier for the military, and the figure with the hat representing the educated classes: the teachers, civil servants, doctors, etc. It's a piece of folk art typical of the Third Republic, dating to somewhere between 1870 and the First World War. This period was the beginning of industrial development, of the recognition of the labour force, of workers and of craftsmanship, which perhaps explains the increase in folk art that was produced during this time. There is a political character to the picture of course, it was evidently made by a republican. The Second Empire ended with the abdication of Napoleon III in 1870 following his defeat in the Franco-Prussian war. This piece was made just after the Paris Commune, when there was ongoing political unrest.'

Remix Gallery
Marché Paul Bert
Allée 6, Stand 91
www.remixgallery.fr
@remixgallerydesign

Eighties design and furniture;
Philippe Starck

VALÉRIE BOUVIER & ANTOINE NOUVET

Domestic Monument – Sinerpica lamp by Michele de Lucchi, Studio Alchimia, 1978. 'Even though we mainly present French design, Italy played a central role in the 80s design revolution, with designers including Ettore Sottsass, Alessandro Mendini, and Michele de Lucchi. They wanted to break the rule book, bringing lots of colour, pattern, and materials, to create forms that were extremely exuberant, that broke down the opposition between what is good and bad taste. Prior to Memphis, Ettore Sottsass and Michele de Lucchi were part of Studio Alchimia, that wanted, just like Memphis Milano did, to shake up what they considered to be a bourgeois vision of design. Alessandro Mendini spoke about some of these creations as 'domestic monuments', which is to say, he wanted to bring a bit of art into the home through design. This lamp is an object, a sculpture, before it's a lamp. It's very joyful, very playful, very colourful. A lamp without a lampshade, a lamp that almost looks like a toy.'

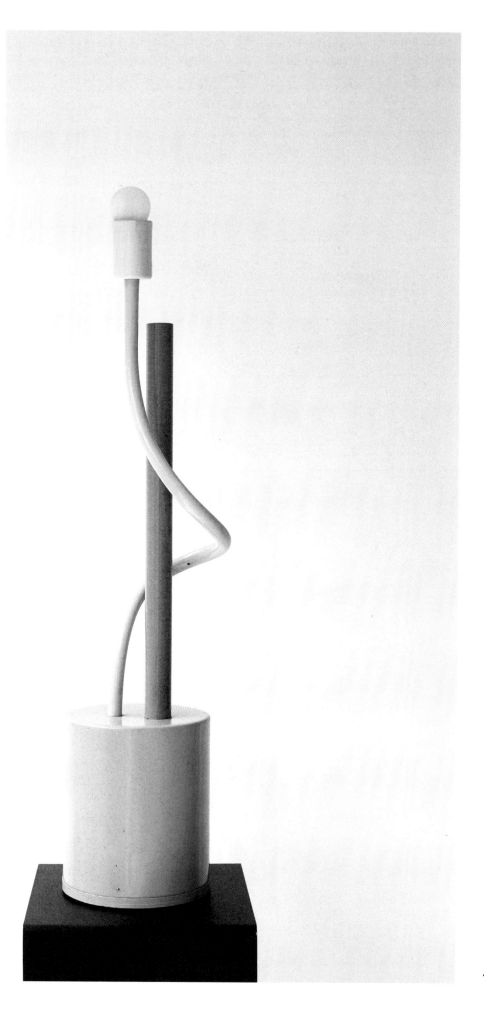

Valerie Bouvier & Antoine Nouvet

46

Signature Piece – 'The Miss Dorn is one of the first chairs we bought when we opened in 2015. Philippe Starck designed this chair in 1981. He names all his designs, and Miss Dorn is a character from Philip K. Dick's science fiction novel, *Ubik*. Starck also called his first design studio Ubik. At the time, Starck was better known as a decorator. He had designed several nightclubs in Paris, notably Les Bains Douches in 1978. When he designed the Starck Club in Dallas in 1984, he chose this chair as its sort of emblem. We are interested in this piece for all these reasons. Its shape too – its line is almost perfect. It's so simple, it's so refined, and so efficient. It references Charlotte Perriand's Revolving Armchair (1928), with the rounded back, but the stiff tripod legs completely break its curved silhouette.'

Who are you?

V: I was born the day Elvis Presley died. I have always loved hoarding and collecting (the dealer's disease!). Before moving to the Puces, I was a visual artist and singer. I met Antoine in 2005 and we've never been apart for more than 72 hours since that day! We started to *chiner* together, which allowed us to buy pieces that we liked for our apartment. And then eventually ... the collectors became dealers.

What does *chiner* mean?

V: It's a game. *Chiner* is exciting and fun at the same time. You go on an adventure and never know what you'll find or what you'll come home with. It can also be frustrating if you are too slow and you miss an object. So you need to be responsive, fast and discerning.

Why the Puces?

V: We wanted to be part of this little village, to participate in the buzz and the hustle and bustle, it seemed obvious to us to establish ourselves here. It is a lively and enchanted place, with such history and charm, which attracts the whole world, from Paris Hilton to Pharrell Williams, from my next-door neighbour to ... everyone comes to the Puces! Spending a day here is a delightful moment, outside of time (except when it rains).

Tell us about your stand.

V: At the Puces since 2015, we specialize in 80s design and we love setting up our stand and changing the decor and colour scheme. We have favourite designers like Philippe Starck, who was the first designer we championed eight years ago; Christian Duc, to whom we dedicated an exhibition of around forty pieces two years ago, and on whom we are preparing a book; Alessandro Mendini, whose work fascinates us; but also many others, such as Andrée Putman, whose timeless aspect we appreciate, or French designers like Gilles Derain and Jean-Michel Wilmotte.

Your favourite historical period?

V: The 80s of course, because they were amazing, trendy, fast, innovative, hypercreative, electronic, and the beginning of the digital age. But we really like the 20s and 30s too, for their modernity, and the manner in which architects conceived of total interiors and reflected on how to live.

Where does your inspiration come from?

V: I grew up in the 80s and back then, television and advertising had a very important role in the home. Each new ad was a micro-event and they were often extremely creative. My inspirations are therefore strongly impregnated by this 'Jean-Paul Goude' aesthetic, by this sometimes quite dark sense of humour. I'm thinking of 'Les Nuls', of Les Rita Mitsouko video clips, of Madonna in the Gaultier cone-bra corset. I'm thinking of the Lee Cooper ads, of Benetton, of the movie *Subway* ...

Who is your hero?

V: Philippe Starck, of course. We love his genius and his folly, and sometimes the two combined; he has a kind of playful madness, he has fun, with no barriers. He has visions, like when you're a child and you make a train out of a pig! There's an inventor side to him, where everything is possible. His father was an aeronautical engineer, and perhaps he gave him a taste for designing and inventing. Starck is always one step ahead of his time: prior to the 80s, he was asking himself about democratic design, accessible to all; in the 90s and early 2000s he began to look at sustainable design, at eco-responsibility. Then in the 2000s, 2010s, he made a chair called A.I. Right now he's working on projects that we could take to space. Starck is protean, he is at once designer, architect, decorator, engineer.

What are you most proud of?

V: When we created Remix Gallery in 2015, 80s design was little known, even a little forgotten, and practically absent from the twentieth-century design market. But we were convinced of its strength, formal qualities and historical significance. Nearly ten years have passed and today we can see the emergence of a real interest in the 1980s, confirmed by the exhibition on the decade which took place at the Musée des Arts Décoratifs in Paris in 2023.

Are you more tradition or revolution?

V: Revolution of course! We are interested in a period and in designers who, in addition to narrating their era through their creations, totally disrupted and influenced our way of life through design.

What is unique about your practice?

V: We do everything, from A to Z! We source the pieces, we are salespeople, scenographers, documentalists, researchers, accountants, communication directors, transporters, delivery men, painters, electricians, and sometimes even relationship therapists!

Does research and documentation take up a lot of your time?

V: It's a huge part of our job! We are also very lucky to be able to meet the participants from this period and to exchange ideas with them on these subjects, which provides us with lots of material and information about the time, the design companies, the fairs, the designers etc.

Have the internet and social networks changed the way you work?

V: The internet is an extraordinary tool that allows us to go where we physically cannot, but it also creates a kind of laziness, because many pieces can be found online and the physical process of going to see an object, to touch it, disappears a little. It's a shame in a way, with good or bad surprises in store. And the internet is a formidable competitor, not always honest ... But let's not talk about the sales platforms that have zero expertise.

Your favourite tool?

V: An electric drill – we use it constantly; and a sponge and Marseille soap, it cleans absolutely everything.

You wouldn't be where you are without ...?

V: My mother, who was an antique dealer and who passed on, with great joy and creativity, her love of this profession to me. And my brother Jean-Baptiste Bouvier, an antique dealer who has supported us so much in our project – which seemed like such a long shot in the beginning.

A secret about the flea market?

V: There are no fleas!

Valerie Bouvier & Antoine Nouvet

48

Design Evolution – 'Starck's Royalton Bar Stool (1988) came a little later, and we see Starck's design evolving, becoming more organic. He designed another piece around the same time, the W.W. stool (1988), for Wim Wenders, that has this organic shape as well, like a rhizome, a plant coming out of the ground. The stool was designed specifically for the Royalton hotel in New York, commissioned by Ian Schrager, co-founder of Studio 54. He's an incredible guy, he invented this mega-club in New York, and then created this iconic hotel. The entire place was meant to be one monumental work by Starck. That's why we like this stool so much, because of its form, and also because it refers to such an iconic place.'

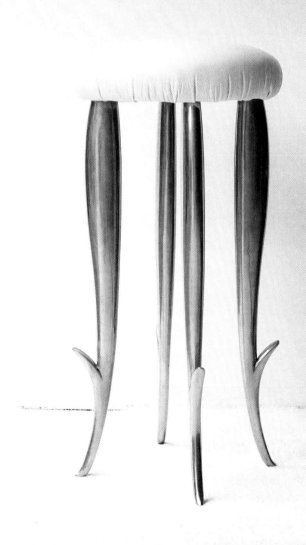

Microtheatre – 'It's still the 80s, but this is something else altogether. Pierre Sala was a man of the theatre: a director and set designer who little by little started designing furniture. He wanted his furniture to be like little plays, micro-shows. The work is very joyful, very spectacular and the pieces are all very limited editions, numbered to 250 pieces maximum. The Piranha chair was his most famous design. Pierre Sala's career as a designer was dazzling in the sense that he was successful very early on, and was soon entrusted with a number of projects, notably the café of the Cartier Foundation in 1985. His career, which was very transgressive, very playful, very colourful, ended abruptly when he died in 1989. In 2023, we presented, in association with three other dealers, an exhibition dedicated to Pierre Sala, the first since his death.'

Valerie Bouvier & Antoine Nouvet

The Secret Life of the Puces —
'As important as the restorer of wood or
ceramics, Balthazar of La Bulle [bubble
wrap] is a key character at the Puces.
His service of custom-made packaging
and packaging materials, and presentation
stands and accessories, is an essential one.
If an overseas customer wants to buy a
chair on a whim, but doesn't have a carrier,
or has no idea how to get their chair to
New York, you can call Balthazar and he'll
build a custom crate. Plus, he's a great guy
who loves hyper-intense techno. If he didn't
exist, we'd have to invent him.'

Living History – If nothing remains (except its bestselling furniture) of the mythic Café Costes, Paris's place-to-be that helped cement Starck's career when it opened on the Place des Innocents in 1984, the Christian de Portzamparc-designed Café Beaubourg, facing the Centre Pompidou and its magic piazza, remains, exactly as it was when it opened in 1987. The monument to 'Postmodern' architecture, with its spectacular stairway, columns and peristyle, and expansive terrace furnished with Portzamparc's cult 'Kaer Bog' armchair, still channels a singular mood particular to the 80s, of festive despair, of dancing in the ruins.

History Lesson — 'Claude Dumas is a
French ceramicist, initially a sculptor,
then at the very beginning of the 80s, he
began making objects in series. In 2002,
he created the ceramic sculpture workshop
at the Beaux-Arts in Paris, which he directs
and where he teaches today. Between 83
and 89, he made vases and bowls, each
one named with a letter of the alphabet.
In 89 — it is one of his last vases — Dumas
produced the W vase, representing the
Chernobyl catastrophe of 1986, in glazed
ceramic. When we did an exhibition on his
work, he was kind enough to bring out his
moulds, and reproduce this vase, which
was impossible to find on the market.
We are incredibly lucky to work with him,
and to learn all the history. If we hadn't
met him, we would never have known that
the W vase was a response to Chernobyl.'

Valerie Bouvier & Antoine Nouvet

Le I

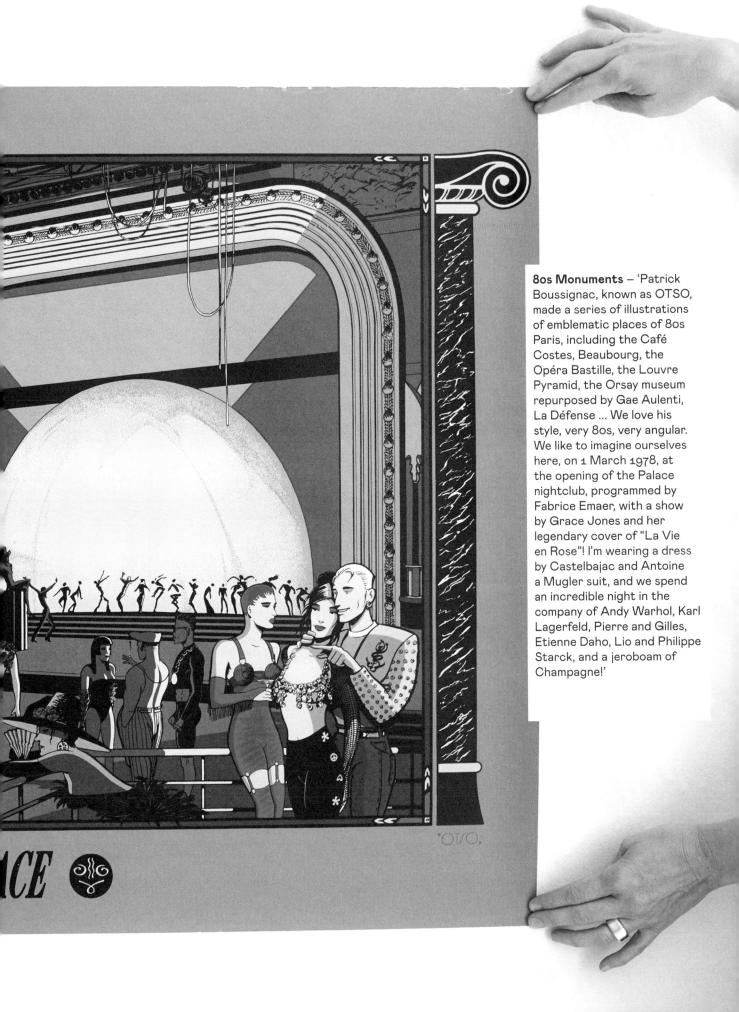

80s Monuments – 'Patrick Boussignac, known as OTSO, made a series of illustrations of emblematic places of 80s Paris, including the Café Costes, Beaubourg, the Opéra Bastille, the Louvre Pyramid, the Orsay museum repurposed by Gae Aulenti, La Défense … We love his style, very 80s, very angular. We like to imagine ourselves here, on 1 March 1978, at the opening of the Palace nightclub, programmed by Fabrice Emaer, with a show by Grace Jones and her legendary cover of "La Vie en Rose"! I'm wearing a dress by Castelbajac and Antoine a Mugler suit, and we spend an incredible night in the company of Andy Warhol, Karl Lagerfeld, Pierre and Gilles, Etienne Daho, Lio and Philippe Starck, and a jeroboam of Champagne!'

PHILIPPE STARCK

Creator, explorer, artistic director,
architect, designer
www.starck.com

I have never lived in cities. I am a man of nature. However,
when I am in Paris, I love to walk, to explore the streets
from Trocadero to the Puces; passing through the inter-
mediate zones, the unknown streets, the outskirts.
I wander through the heart of the Puces de Saint-Ouen,
soaking up this distinctive culture. I fell in love with it, not
so much for the sake of looking for some object, although
I often discovered extraordinary ones that told strange
stories, enigmas, but for the love of its society. It's the
society of the Puces that I love, and that I dream of belonging to. I listen to snatches of conversation between the
merchants, looking for fertile surprises, accidents, stam-
merings, dreams that could create my own ...

One day, I found a chair from the 1960s, pale turquoise
and white, with one half of the seat shorter than the other.
I bought it just so I could imagine what kind of person
would have needed this custom-made chair. After much
observation, I deduced that it was the chair of a cello or
harp player in an orchestra. But it could also be the chair
of a person missing a leg. It's this kind of puzzle that I like
to solve, through my imaginary solutions.

The Puces is nothing other than a totally successful
mini, organic city, where humans trade with culture, intelligence, spirit and friendship. It is a nano-prototype of
the memory of a forgotten society that could once again
become an inspiring model. For as long as I can remember, I have dreamed of having a stand there, just like those
merchants. This intention has never left me.

Philippe and Jasmine Starck photographed at
Mob House, a hotel designed by Starck in Saint-Ouen.

sentimentale fx
Marché Paul Bert
Allée 1, Stand 108
@sentimental_fx

Design and art, vintage and contemporary

FRANÇOIS-XAVIER COURRÈGES

What is your expertise, speciality or particularity?
I specialize in design from the 1980s to 2000, mainly Italian and French, with a particular focus on the work of Gaetano Pesce, which I like to contrast with the Belgian, Maarten Van Severen's, minimal style. I also show some slightly older pieces, such as lighting by Gino Sarfatti or André Cazenave, as well as contemporary pieces. And coming from a contemporary art background, I quite naturally wanted to present some editions and ephemera by painters I like, such as Elizabeth Peyton, Brian Calvin or Cédric Rivrain, with whom I am preparing a collaboration.

Tell us about your profession.
When I was working as an artist, I appreciated the field of possibilities that opened up to me, this great freedom, particularly when making videos. It allowed me to combine different disciplines that I liked. I get a similar feeling with this activity. I choose to show a particular object, to associate it with another, and yet another, to develop a setting, to construct an image. In short, it's very creative.

How did you get where you are?
I opened my stand at Paul Bert in the spring of 2022 after practising this activity on the side for years. I have been passionate about design since adolescence and my style has been shaped over time and of course continues to evolve. My first acquisitions were ceramics by Jacques Blin bought at the Paul Bert market when I was 18, then I bought a lot of 70s design, doubtless out of nostalgia. Today, although each object has its history and belongs to a part of the history of design, I like the idea that it can be timeless.

How does the Puces relate to the larger antiques and second-hand market in Paris, and around the world?
It's a place where trends emerge. The dealers come from all walks of life, each with a personal proposition, each with their own way of working. In fact, we don't even all do the same job, as everyone approaches it and practises it in different ways. We don't define ourselves in the same way either: antique dealer, second-hand dealer, decorator, dealer, gallerist, archivist … Consequently, it's rich in eclecticism and quality. The Puces is a renowned place and occupies an essential role in the international market for antiques and vintage design. Thus, we benefit from great visibility which attracts collectors and enthusiasts from all over the world.

What does *chiner* mean?
As a dealer, it's the basis of our work. Again, I think that everyone has their own methodology, their own approach. It's about finding the objects that best match your aesthetic; it's part of the creative process. It's by doing it regularly that you learn to know the merchandise, refine your taste and open yourself up to new discoveries.

Your best find?
I can't say that it's my best find because many acquisitions make me happy, but I remain very attached to a wall lamp in the form of a ceramic shirt with a plexiglass tie. It was designed by J. C. Peiré, a prolific designer – though inconsistent in my opinion – of functional decorative objects in ceramic of the 70s and 80s. It was the starting point for me in my research of his work and of French design of the 80s.

What has, or hasn't, changed at the Puces?
I'll answer with this line by Jean-Paul Sartre, from *Nausea*, 'Nothing has changed and yet everything exists in a different way.' Dealers come and go over time, fashions evolve.

Is there an image from the past that obsesses or inspires you?
My childhood and my adolescence and all the roads travelled, the memories that I reactivate with documents from that time, between the 1970s and the 1990s.

Why the name?
Sentimental is a word that describes me well and which echoes the artistic work which I have developed in the past around the feeling of love, its related states, on memory and remembrance. Associated with the initials of my first name, it became a nickname, and the name of my business based on my passion for design. I like this name which can be understood with multiple meanings in both French and English.

If you weren't at the Puces, where would you be?
Silver Lake. It's a place I think about often. To wander through it is really inspiring. There's something about the Modernist architecture, the vegetation, the light … the light is really specific to Los Angeles. Everything appears really cinematographic. It's a neighbourhood where you see Hollywood, you know, the letters H O L L Y W O O D, on the hill. When I daydream, I can totally imagine settling down there.

François-Xavier Courrèges

Personal Work — 'Two stills from a video I made, *Le Sentiment d'aventure* (2011). The title is a reference to what Jean-Paul Sartre writes about in *Nausea* — the irreversibility of time. In the video, the foot is an ice sculpture that melts away like time itself. And the foot, moulded on my own, is a tribute to Gaetano Pesce's UP7 lounge chair.'

Solo Show – 'A view of my stand with a selection of pieces by Gaetano Pesce. I only ever present a few pieces at a time, showcasing them through mini exhibitions, which evolve as pieces come and go. I seek to establish correspondence between objects, to create enveloping and coherent worlds. In this way, these presentations are more like installations, informed by my experience and my sensibility as an artist. I am very selective and only choose pieces that really fascinate me, rare, sometimes unusual objects, and one-offs. I strive to discover and show pieces that are difficult to find. I favour objects with a sculptural dimension, pieces of furniture whose notion of functionality can be called into question. I am interested in trompe l'oeil, anthropomorphic shapes, but also objects with simple and minimal lines.'

François-Xavier Courrèges

62

Artist Ephemera – 'When you really like an artist, especially a very famous artist, like Elizabeth Peyton, it's usually hard to acquire a piece unfortunately. Multiples are sometimes available, and beyond that there are all sorts of little things that circulate, things like autographed photos, postcards, books, sometimes it's a small drawing, or a letter. They're like little unexpected finds, things that you glean at random, outside of the traditional gallery circuit. They are objects which are not intended to be nor are considered works of art, per se, but which somehow become them.'

Bonnefantenmuseum Maastricht

Elizabeth Peyton
18.10.09 - 21.03.10

Back from Oblivion – 'Brezza Note table lamps by Andrea Anastasio. Anastasio is an Italian designer who is not that well known. He created this series for Artemide at the end of the 90s. I think these lamps are really beautiful. I really like the aluminium, I like its relationship with the tulle. I have realised that this lamp is a bit of a forgotten piece, we seldom see it – I suppose it wasn't produced for long. I love showing things that we never see, or see rarely, or not enough. Though you have to stock up as much as possible before starting to communicate, because afterwards the prices can rise. I'm careful about posting an item, especially on Instagram.'

Comeback – Pierre Sala, Mikado shelving unit, aluminium and lacquered wood, 1984. 'I joined forces with three other dealers – Jean-Philippe Mercier, Remix Gallery and Hugo Abraham – to present the first monographic exhibition of French designer Pierre Sala, who had fallen into obscurity since his early death in 1989. The exhibition, held in early 2023 in Paris, was the result of intensive research, both for the exhibited pieces and the documentation and archives relating to his life and work. Research is an important and exciting part of my work. This shelving unit is really super-ingenious – everything is misaligned and asymmetrical, yet it is sturdy and the shelves are perfectly straight.'

Noodle Art – 'Macaroni trivet, and farfalle rigate bowl by Chris Fusaro, a Canadian designer who lives and works in Milan. He was an assistant at Gaetano Pesce's workshop in Brooklyn before branching out on his own. His series Pasta Persa (2022–23) is the result of experiments motivated by a desire to make kitchenware out of pasta! The process relies on a unique combination of silversmithing and foundry techniques to produce handcrafted, one-of-a-kind, functional sculptures for the kitchen. Made entirely of bronze using lost wax casting, *cera persa* in Italian, each piece is nickel plated to resist exposure to water, oil and heat.'

Sentimental Value – 'I grew up in Paris, very close to the Tristan Tzara House (1925–26) by Adolf Loos on Avenue Junot. As a child, it intrigued me a lot, its façade seemed incongruous and austere. I had difficulty understanding it and had fun imagining the configuration of its interior spaces. It was my first encounter with modern architecture, of which I became a fervent fan over the years.'

13. BOULEVARD SAINT DENIS · 3ème ÉTAGE
75002 PARIS

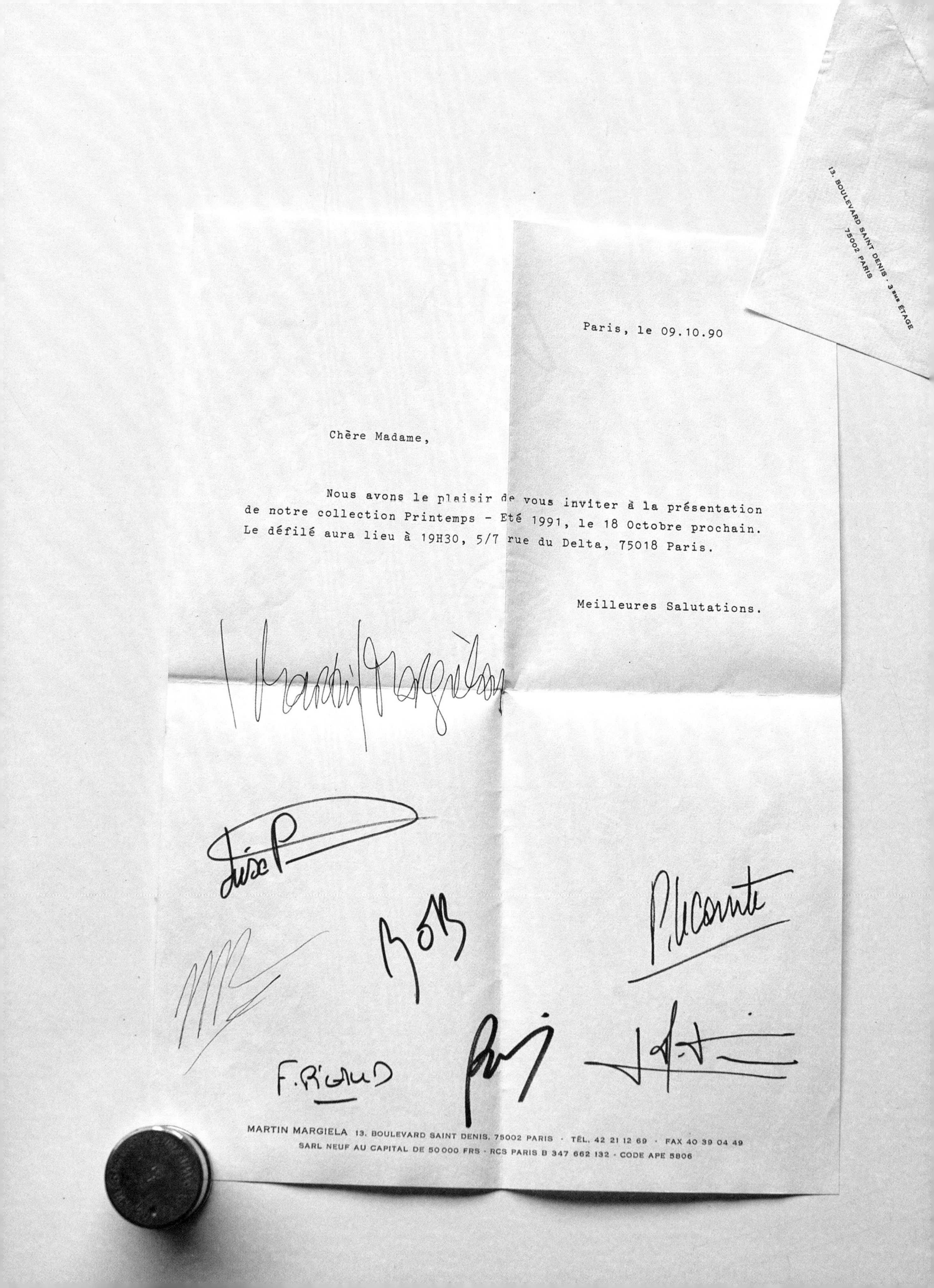

Paris, le 09.10.90

Chère Madame,

Nous avons le plaisir de vous inviter à la présentation de notre collection Printemps - Eté 1991, le 18 Octobre prochain. Le défilé aura lieu à 19H30, 5/7 rue du Delta, 75018 Paris.

Meilleures Salutations.

MARTIN MARGIELA 13. BOULEVARD SAINT DENIS, 75002 PARIS · TÉL. 42 21 12 69 · FAX 40 39 04 49
SARL NEUF AU CAPITAL DE 50 000 FRS · RCS PARIS B 347 662 132 · CODE APE 5806

Watershed – 'A photo I took in October 1990, when I was a teenager, at one of the first Martin Margiela shows in Paris. Margiela was just emerging at that time, starting a revolution in the fashion world. The presentation took place at dusk in an abandoned car park in the 18th arrondissement. Many guests, all standing, filled the space, and when the first models appeared, people shouted "Careful! Get out of the way!" so that the girls could make their way through the crowd, leaving in their wake the smell of patchouli. The music was loud, 70s rock. It was a happening, and we were all part of it. It was an intense moment, and the images stayed with me for a long time. The experience influenced my taste. I still have the invitation too, typewritten, and signed by Martin Margiela and the rest of the team.'

De Laurentis Paris
Marché Paul Bert,
Allée 1, Stands 112 & 114
@de_laurentis_paris
www.delaurentisparis.com

Contemporary, avant-garde, vintage fashion

MAXIME DE LAURENTIS

Power dressing – 'Comme des Garçons 1988 ensemble in beige wool with red stripes, consisting of a bolero with balloon sleeves closing with a double button connected by a chain, and a long skirt with asymmetrical cut-outs and darts. We're in full "power dressing" era here, and Rei Kawakubo approaches this trend with an even more distinctive shoulder. Moreover, it's part of a pivotal collection demonstrating a marked shift towards conceptualism, which will become increasingly radical, season after season. I'm particularly attached to the entire collection, as well as the photos for the campaign taken by Peter Lindbergh in a factory in Nancy, with Kanako B. Koga styling. Kanako subsequently worked with Martin at Hermès and Maison Martin Margiela. The story of the piece's provenance also touches me – it belonged to a person I met in 2016 in a particular period of my life with an incredible wardrobe that marked my career. I can't say more ;-)'

Tell us about your stand.
Since 2011, I have had a stand at the Paul Bert market where I sell vintage clothes and accessories. Here, I represent designers of the 80s, 90s and 2000s who can be described as 'avant-garde' or 'minimalist': Yohji Yamamoto, Martin Margiela, Rei Kawakubo, Helmut Lang, Jil Sander, Junya Watanabe ...

How did you get where you are?
I didn't grow up with these clothes. Coming from the south of France, I had a much more Latin education, the brands I knew, that I saw, that were in fashion, were Dolce & Gabbana, Versace, or Chanel. But my first job in fashion was as an intern at Margiela. Then I stayed on as assistant stylist, then stylist ... I stayed for almost eight years at Margiela, with Martin. It was an education that really changed my perception of fashion, and this relationship to clothing marked me for life. Martin's creative process was really very natural, which proves that he's someone who, psychically, is truly an artist.

Why the Puces?
It's part of my upbringing, I am the son and grandson of antique furniture dealers. Since childhood, I have wandered second-hand shops and flea markets, so it's a familiar environment that is essential to my well-being. And flea markets and second-hand pieces were always a tool and a source of inspiration when I was a stylist. So it is the synthesis of both things.

What is a typical day for you at the Puces?
I have an unchanging routine. First, say hello to the other dealers and neighbours who we'll be spending the day with. Then 'raise the curtain' and set up and light the stand. I can't work if I haven't swept. And lastly I burn sage or palo santo in every corner of my stand. This is the framework, the rest of the day is improvisation according to encounters.

How are your pieces restored?
I have a very specific protocol. All the pieces are dry-heated then steamed and then photographed. This is when I identify the need to repair the piece, or to leave the mark or patina of time. I don't make any alterations, it's just a matter of fixing the linings, or replacing a button if necessary, so that it can live on with its new family. My stand is a kind of little two-storey house, the result of several stands joined together, so I am lucky to have a floor where I can photograph and store, protected from ultraviolet radiation, the nine hundred pieces that make up my archive.

What professions do you work with?
There is an 'off market' of pieces that don't transit through the Puces but that we dealers have nevertheless sourced and that we present directly to our customers. B2B represents 70 per cent of my activity, whether it be with fashion houses, institutions, other dealers, collectors, foreign shops, or stylists for cinema.

What is unique about your practice?
I approach fashion in a rather singular way because I do not necessarily look for a purchase as an end in itself but more as a pathway to knowledge.

I have a time machine; where do we go?
Haussmann's Paris of the Second Empire, 1870. I'm really obsessed with the beginning of the industrialization of fashion. And with Charles Frederick Worth, who invented Parisian haute couture; he created the principle of the couture house with the couturier as a creative force ... before, we just went to a seamstress to have a garment or a nice outfit made. He had influential clients, like the Empress Eugénie. And, I really like Haussmannian architecture too. I like the rigidity, the linearity. I'm not from Paris, so the city's aesthetic is exotic for me.

What makes the Puces unique?
The Puces is and forms a junction point, an agora, a crossroads, where many actors from different social backgrounds meet, dealers as well as visitors. And it's the hub where all the goods transit, physically or virtually, because some dealers now use other platforms such as online sales or auction rooms. So it is the synergy of merchants and their wares that makes the Puces unique. You have to come to see both.

Does the Puces make the world a better place?
The fact is that it's free of cars, which encourages the visitor to slow down and wander. And there is now a new clientele more focused on ecological issues, wanting to buy better, proof that the Puces is not just the place where trends are made and unmade, but is anchored in something deeper.

Have the internet and social networks changed the way you work?
I obviously use social networks and I also have a website. But they are not very important; I post once a week. I prefer to arouse desire by creating tension, and encouraging customers to come to visit me. In addition, my pieces are sourced from private wardrobes, so are available second-hand for the first time. I don't want to reveal everything flatly online.

What does *chiner* mean?
It's the search for a piece of furniture, object, or anything else. It can be precise, with something in mind that motivates the search, or much more open, with the quest for a Eureka moment, a jolt that provokes an emotion, a desire, or even a compulsion/repulsion. It's an exercise in concentration, because hundreds of visual stimuli come into play.

Your best find?
There are many, and they are usually still associated with their first owner. I serve as a go-between. I strive to unearth pieces every day. I don't want to reduce them to their aesthetic or market values, because all the garments in my shop have value in my eyes. And I never buy the same piece twice, in order to offer my clients an experience that is always different.

What inspires you?
I don't watch what other people do, nor do I have a muse. I constantly reinvent myself without looking at what is happening around me. I'm kind of like a satellite that circles the planet Mode. This position suits me very well.

Lucky Find – 'A brooch of YSL's famous logo by Cassandre. I bought it in the late 90s with my dad at the Puces for 5 francs from a "*biffin*". *Biffins* are people who scavenge stuff – they'll find a scarf, then sell it – and are allowed to sell off the ground in a zone on the edge of the Puces. This is what's called a circular economy!'

Sentimental Value – 'Tom Ford-era Gucci, hooded jacket in black nylon lined with mesh, 1999. It was a gift from my father who found it at a flea market in Hyères, in the south of France. He must have paid like 10 francs at the time; the zip is broken. He knew that I loved Gucci. Now, strangely, Tom Ford's Gucci is really coming back into fashion.'

Voodoo – 'Like jewellery, clothes conserve the energy of the previous owners, so I burn sage or palo santo to drive out the spirits, so that only the stylistic power of the cut remains; this is very, very important.'

Trade Secret – 'My collection of lookbooks and fashion magazines is an important tool that helps me date pieces. Some brands' codes – the codes inside clothes – are really hard to crack; Yohji Yamamoto for example is very difficult to decipher. When I can't crack the code, I refer to lookbooks. It's the difference between saying "it's a pretty white jacket, very well cut" and giving the precise material, the season, its number in the running order on the catwalk … these details are priceless. There's style.com and Vogue Runway too, but they're not very well digitized. I spend several hours a day on documentation and research, which means I am constantly learning. In order to be competent and professional in what we do, this is essential. In addition, "storytelling" is an important part of the business — it can trigger a sale.'

Maxime de Laurentis

77

Museum Piece – 'This is the S/S 1994 reissue of the Margiela "tattoo" mesh top from 1989. For the house's fifth anniversary, Martin Margiela celebrated with a retrospective of the best designs from each season and decided to redo the tattoo top which was such a hit at the brand's first show. Ink-coloured tribal tattoo designs are printed on a flesh-coloured synthetic mesh. Trompe l'oeil is a founding theme of the house and was experimented with in many forms for almost 20 years, and continues to be, despite the change of artistic direction. The piece is in the collections of many fashion museums, including the Met, Palais Galliera, and the Museum of Kyoto.'

Maxime de Laurentis

78

Showpiece – 'Extra-long, midnight blue Maison Martin Margiela overcoat in felted wool from the winter 1989 collection that I will probably never sell. Though it is often on loan; I get asked for it a lot. Made by Deni Cler in Mantua, this double-breasted coat with hidden buttons borrows the cut of narrow shouldered jackets, with a prominent "cigarette" detail. It could be styled with a roll of brown tape instead of a belt.'

Fake News – 'Unfortunately, the entire section of the Puces that runs along the ring road which was once dedicated to trinkets, second-hand clothes, and American military surplus, has been replaced by counterfeit clothing. It's very organized. There are containers that arrive every week; we're talking millions in turnover. Simon Jacquemus posted a video of himself on Instagram here holding a fake Jacquemus bag. He took it as a joke, but this trade represents serious losses for the industry. These two parallel worlds do not communicate, there is no crossover, either by the dealers or the visitors. Which is a shame because before, people who came to buy trinkets or second-hand clothes also came to marvel at the other markets, even if it was not within their budget. And this divide can be confusing for people visiting the Puces for the first time, because you have to traverse this barrier to get to our market.'

Furniture and ceramic art

NATHALIE DUPUIS

Tell us about your stand.

On my stand you find principally furniture from the 50s to the 80s and 'art ceramics', from the 50s to the present day. Art ceramics are the opposite of utilitarian ceramics. They are ceramics with no other function than to be an objet d'art. They can be pictorial or sculptural. Pictorial when the ceramicist works mainly with glazes, and sculptural when they work more specifically on form.

Why ceramics?

I handled ceramics a lot when I worked at the Musèe des Arts Decoratifs and liked it. And before that I had written a historiographical thesis on sculpture, which talked a lot about nineteenth-century collectors in France, but through the Renaissance Florentine sculptor Donatello, so I never really separated art and decorative arts. You can't put everything in little boxes, it's a continuum, the history of art, and the history of objects. Now we talk about 'art' ceramics – they're no longer utilitarian objects, and artists express themselves a lot, especially today, which is why contemporary ceramics interest me.

Your favourite artist?

As in music, there is so much artistic production, from antiquity to the present day, that in my opinion it's important to understand how to simply marvel at what we find beautiful. I have no absolute favourite, although in ceramics, I admire the work of Jean-Joseph Carriès. His work is very strong, on an emotional level. He suffered a lot in his childhood, and he expresses this in a way, we sense that he is tormented. His work can be a little weird or disturbing, and at the same time, it's very beautiful, and for the time, very modern; it dates to around 1880, before Art Nouveau. For me he is one of the first to make such powerful art ceramics. For example, his contemporary, Théodore Deck, worked in a completely different register, less disturbing, more in tune with the times.

Your best find?

My first major purchase at Drouot was a large piece from Jean Derval's early work. As soon as I saw it I said to myself 'It's a Jean Derval!', but I was with a ceramics expert friend who didn't agree. I took a photo of the signature and googled it and discovered that it was his original signature when he started in Saint-Armand-en-Puisaye with Pierre Pigaglio, who had taken over Carriès' studio; it was his first studio before moving to Vallauris. I was very proud to have recognized a piece by Jean Derval, intuitively I knew that it was him, I don't know why, there was a power, which hit me in the face. It's always very satisfying, to make your brain work, and your eye, to manage to give a name to a piece that could remain anonymous, be lost.

How did you get where you are?

I studied art history for five years, then I worked for an art history website until it closed after the stock market crash, like so many start-ups at the time. After that, I worked for Phaidon University Press as a copy editor, and then I did an internship at the Musée des Arts Décoratifs. They called me a year later when a position became available in the inventory department. I spent three years there, then ten years in conservation. The Musée des Arts Décoratifs is unique in France because it covers all periods, from the Middle Ages to today. It has very fine collections. It was a private museum at the beginning, established in 1882 by a group of collectors, before moving into the Marsan wing of the Louvre in 1905.

What makes the Puces unique?

We are surrounded by objects every day at the Puces, and there are a lot of things that I never see in a museum, because not everything enters museums. Museums must make choices, there are very strict acquisition policies. Whereas the art market is completely free, so dealers have great freedom, they decide what they want on show, they take liberties which can also influence acquisitions, it's a circle. There is no museum without an antique dealer, and no antique dealer without a museum, and if you look at how a museum acquires pieces and where they come from, they once passed through the hands of a dealer or a collector, or both.

Do you have to be a bit crazy to work at the Puces?

No, but you need personality and a certain maturity (if you are not the daughter or son of a dealer). You have to know how to observe and respect many unwritten rules that are passed down from generation to generation. There are ethics, and reputations are made very quickly, in both a positive as well as a negative sense.

What are you most proud of?

I don't know if I would say proud, but I'm very satisfied to be able to do what I love, to have the freedom of my choices, and of my taste. It's really very fortunate. I'm also proud of the response I have, of the enthusiasm from clients who buy and who buy again from me, and that we manage to connect aesthetically. It's encouraging, it's rewarding. I didn't expect that – to have such positive feedback from customers, but also recognition from dealers. There are a lot of us, and I was quickly included in the group. It's nice.

Does the Puces make the world a better place?

In a sense it is an ecological market. We restore, upcycle and resell old products that are therefore not destroyed and do not clutter bins.

I have a time machine; where do we go?

I'd start from scratch at the Puces but with all the knowledge I have today, to avoid all the mistakes I've made. As we work alone and we learn by doing, I learned things that I would avoid doing again. I'd go slower. I'd put aside certain pieces which today have become impossible to find, which have become historical pieces, and which will only become more so.

Nathalie Dupuis

Organic Forms – Unglazed stoneware piece, early 70s. Hildegund Schlichenmaier. 'Deeply influenced by Jean and Jacqueline Lerat, who introduced her to wood firing in La Borne, this German-born ceramicist moved to Redan, France, in 1969. Her work is both sculptural and organic, with elements seeming to belong to both the plant and animal kingdoms, to have been formed over millennia, like fossils or the seabed. Some of her works have entered national collections, including the National Manufacture de Sèvres, and the Musée des Arts Decoratifs in Paris.'

Ancestor Worship – *Hommage aux ancêtres*, Eukeni Callejo, 2021. Mixed clay, porcelain slip. 'A Basque potter who settled in Bordeaux, Callejo fell in love with pottery from the age of 20, training at the art school in Bilbao between 1983 and 1986. His production is mainly sculptural, even including the limited number of bowls he makes. His current work is very mineral, his pieces evoke nature, lava, burnt wood. The porcelain slip that partially covers the overfired clay until it deforms, brings light and emphasizes the shapes.'

School of Life – 'The Marché de Vanves is important to me, it's where I learned the art of *chiner*, where I began to meet people, and also where I mastered the effort of getting up early. It was my school. I live nearby, and I used to come every weekend, to learn to "see". There is so much stuff, but the eye must stop on what is important, and must be fast, if you want to be the first to get your hands on an object or piece of furniture. It's a good exercise. Once I bought a relatively large piece by Mado Jolain which was sitting on a table for ten euros. But it's also where I made mistakes. I bought a fake once, and lost 600 euros. You must learn to be careful, that's part of the education.'

The Secret Life of the Puces – The electrician Marc Jornod has been operating out of a tiny workshop tucked away behind the Marché Biron for over two decades. 'I have a workshop at the heart of the Puces where we restore lighting fixtures of all styles, all periods, but I have a pronounced taste for eighteenth- and nineteenth-century chandeliers. We take care of the cleaning and rewiring of chandeliers. We restore the gilding too. And when they have crystal parts, we repair the individual pieces and harmonise the ensemble, restoring the movement.'

Nathalie Dupuis

Early Work — Ceramic table lamp, c. 1954, André-Aleth Masson. 'Born in Saint-Malo, Masson studied at the Beaux-Arts in Rennes in 1938, at the Beaux-Arts in Paris after the war, and then ceramics at the Collège Fontcarrade (Montpellier). Back in Paris in 1949, he bought his first kiln, and in 1950 his initial pieces were shown at the Salon des Indépendants. While his early work retained a utilitarian aspect, over his career the forms became increasingly freer: more and more sculptural, architectural and voluminous, with explosive colours.'

Sculptural Dimension – *Faille*, 2004, Gisèle Buthod-Garçon. Clay sculpture, refractory glaze, raku firing. 'The exceptional character of Buthod-Garçon's work comes from managing to combine Raku firing technique with very thick glazes. It is a paradox with which she has established her notoriety. The quest for a quality glaze is essential for her. Which is to say, its physicality, depth, transparency and the dynamics of its luminous highlights. This quality is generally obtained at high heat (1,300°C), but she manages to obtain it at low temperatures. The major components of her approach are volumes in space and the sculptural dimension of the pieces she creates. Earth, fire, form, glaze, nature and travel are her sources of inspiration. Her work is of an incredible variety, she never stops experimenting and renewing her style.'

Nathalie Dupuis

Museum Piece – Detail of one of the Period Rooms of the Musèe des Arts Decoratifs in Paris. 'In this Period Room, the decorator François-Joseph Graf has reconstructed the dining room commissioned in 1879 by Charles Gillot from his friend the artist Eugène Grasset for his *hôtel particulier* on Rue Madame in Paris. This room records the phenomenon of the collaboration between artists, dealers and discerning collectors. The earthenware and porcelain pieces that make up this dining room's decor were created by contemporaries of Grasset, such as Théodore Deck, who, between 1860 and 1890, in contact with Japan, China or Turkey, renewed the ceramic and glass arts.'

Natural Resources – Glazed bottle, c. 1990–2000, Alain Gaudebert. 'Alain Gaudebert settled in Saint Amand-en-Puisaye, in Burgundy, about 50 years ago, following the man who inspired him, Jean-Joseph Carriès (1855–1884). The latter, along with Vassil Ivanoff (1897–1973), influenced his way of working, going against the mainstream, breaking the codes of traditional ceramics. Like Ivanoff, he chose to work in stoneware, maintaining its primitive power. Gaudebert innovates, invents, plays with form, glazes, and tames fire. He creates ceramics with flowing, superimposed, chaotic glazes. He masters his technique perfectly and seeks inspiration for his art of earth and fire in painting, sculpture and graphic design, and also nature, a major source of inspiration.'

Nathalie Dupuis

Living History
— A ceramicist's
work space at the
Manufacture de Sèvres
porcelain factory.
'Sèvres was initially a
royal factory, then an
imperial factory, and
today it is a national
factory, and historically
one of the most
important in France.
Sèvres produces
exceptional tableware
and vases, which were
systematically exhibited
at all the Exposition
Universelles — from
the very first one in
London in 1851 — where
it represented French
savoir-faire and technical
excellence. A huge
number of ceramicists
have passed through
Sèvres, it is like a school.'

KARL FOURNIER & OLIVIER MARTY

Architects
Studio KO
www.studioko.fr
oeildeko.com

From the beginning of our practice, we have done as much interior design as architecture, and interior design obviously means furniture, objects, design. The best place to find all that is still the Puces, where everything is brought together in one place. You find all periods, all styles – very old things, and at the same time very recent things; it is incomparably eclectic. In one afternoon, in one morning, you can travel through centuries. And at the Puces, you have direct relationships, both with the object and with the dealers, who are themselves great hunters, *chineurs*. Ultimately, we share a common passion, the passion for the object.

I see something and I like it immediately without knowing why. When I like something, I am a compulsive buyer. But I also buy specific things that don't even have time to pass through my house because they are destined for this or that project. For every project I receive a list of things we are looking for, for a particular room: a particular type of lamp, a particular desk, a particular type of chair, and I go hunting. In the past, designers like Jacques Grange used very few contemporary objects in their decor. Today it's the opposite – typically, everything is chosen from a catalogue, with only 10 per cent of vintage pieces. And I deplore that.

Not all our clients appreciate old things, and we must adapt to their taste, but we always try to avoid a place looking too decorated. We try to give a form of naturalness to our designs, and the only way to achieve that really is to mix all the sources. We always ask our clients, for example, if there is any furniture of their own that they want us to include. This can often even be a starting point. Because it's very important for us that they don't feel as though they are living in a showroom or in a space that we have made to please ourselves, or to create a beautiful spread for a magazine. That they walk in and feel at home. There are things that we can design specifically for a project, obviously there are new things that we can buy, and above all there are vintage pieces that we source, which for me add that little something extra which means that one interior does not resemble another. It's the mix of all these things which in the end gives a particular atmosphere to a place, that's not too easy to interpret, not too predictable.

Karl Fournier and Olivier Marty photographed at their agency in Paris.

Marché Paul Bert
Allée 5, Stand 255
@max_keys

Sourcing unique objects, specializing in
form, function and design

MAX KEYS

Why the Puces?

I came to the Puces from London four years ago while on a romantic weekend in Paris. Imagine a five-year-old going to Disneyland for the first time. I just thought it was absolutely amazing. The simplicity of it, and the juxtaposition of it being in kind of a working-class area but there are millions of pounds of antiques trading hands. I saw a dealer who had just five pieces on his stand. It blew me away, the sheer arrogance that someone could carry such little yet amazing stock! It left me in awe. Three years later I had my stand. I feel really proud to be here, and I've been incredibly welcomed. It's one of the best places on the planet for antiques. I find it quite astonishing that it exists actually. I just don't even think you could come close to recreating that now; I don't see that it would ever be possible to do it elsewhere.

Does the Puces de Saint-Ouen have a sister elsewhere on the planet?

London has kind of died because of all the big chains coming in. Portobello Road is just Starbucks and coffee shops and clothes shops now, and there are very few antiques left. After Brexit, I felt that coming to France was necessary for my career, that I had more opportunity to buy interesting pieces here.

How did you get where you are?

I started out in the business in London as what is called a 'runner'. I used to drive out, buy stuff, then visit galleries or shops, mainly in London, and sell from the back of my van. I could turn up in a really shit van, but if I had beautiful pieces, I was never looked down upon. I learned pretty quickly from doing that. For some reason, I think it's illegal to do this in France, but it's still quite a big thing in London. I did that for a good four years. I used to drive to France, funnily enough, and bring stuff back. I worked solo for years. Though it was always a bit lonely. I found that I was just sitting on the motorway most of the time.

What is unique about your practice?

I have a pretty quirky style. I have always found strength in individual pieces, rather than focusing on a certain period or style. I predominantly buy twentieth-century pieces, but I would gladly buy Renaissance if it had something going for it. I recently sold a Byzantine gold necklace and in the same day bought the most amazing Deco chairs. I'm more interested in items than names and I think the item has to really speak, has to make an immediate statement.

Where does your inspiration come from?

Jacques Grange, David Hicks and Christopher Hodsoll, to name a few. Christopher Hodsoll is a London-based decorator and antique dealer known for his idiosyncratic taste. I've long been a fan of his work. His style has been described as 'decaying grandeur' which I think is a charming way of looking at it. He works with exceptionally expensive items in their original state. Nothing is polished. His properties appear totally effortless, they look like they've been there forever, which I find really amusing. It's kind of old money, but chic. Like, you know when you see old ladies in Paris in the posh neighbourhoods, and they've got this effortless style.

What makes a good dealer in your opinion?

I guess it's a skill-set around finding stuff that other people are not finding.

Do you believe in voodoo?

I used to be more superstitious; I used to have this thing where when I went to a market if I didn't buy something in the first ten minutes I thought I wasn't going to buy much at all. So I'd usually try and spend money immediately when I got there, when it opened.

Do you buy to sell or sell to buy?

I think I'm selling to feed a habit. I literally can't stop buying stuff. I think the selling is the relief, it means I can buy more stuff. I'm like some kind of it-girl who needs to buy new clothes all time.

What does *chiner* mean?

I don't speak much French. But there's an English term which doesn't seem to exist in French. I always really liked the hierarchy in the trade in England, and so at the kind of bottom of the chain, which doesn't exist so much nowadays, I think it's pretty much illegal, but there were people that were referred to as 'knockers', people that would just knock on people's doors and ask if they had any antiques for sale. And they were usually incredibly charismatic and were able to buy all of this stuff from people usually for not a respectable price. It's funny as well, when I used to deal with certain types in the trade, money was always discussed in Cockney rhyming slang; so a 'score' is 20 pounds, 500 pounds is a 'monkey' … Another old term people use, if you go out and buy something for £20 then sell it for £500, we refer to that as a 'touch'. It's kind of insider language; I know I can say stuff to certain types and other people wouldn't have a clue what I'm talking about.

Have the internet and social networks changed the way you work?

When I speak to English dealers, all they do is complain how the internet has ruined everything. It's basically given everyone fair opportunity to research what they have. Before, the knowledge existed because you took the time to read books and talk, so I can understand why they say this. But the internet kind of taught me what I was doing, so I don't have a problem with it. This is the thing, I'm just quite lazy now. I buy all my stuff on the internet, I have a shipper, and I'd much rather be going out, going to *brocantes*, going to shops, going to fairs abroad, but I've just managed to streamline my business so I'm not losing money if I drive to Italy. It's really not as fun, but it works.

Max Keys

Wow Factor — 'Detail from a monumental tin-glazed terracotta abstract mosaic, from the 60s, that I bought in Germany, and it has absolutely no provenance whatsoever. I'm trying to think how to word it so it sounds as amazing as it looks!'

St Ives School – 'Carved out of Portland stone, circa 1960, this sculpture was pulled out of a bush 100 miles away from St Ives in Cornwall, where there was an avant-garde movement post-war centred around Barbara Hepworth, so this piece could potentially have an important name attached to it, but I'm yet to attribute it. I especially like the fact that it's covered in moss.'

Max Keys

Wish List – 'Don Shoemaker for Señal S.A., Hecho, Mexico, circa 1960. Solid rosewood chair with black leather sling upholstery. If you look closely at the seat base, it is on hinges, so it rocks! Just an amazing chair really, and really rare to find them over here, and in exceptional condition. They've been on an imaginary list of items I'd like to own; it took me five years to find a pair.'

Max Keys

Local Hero — Cyril Aouizerate, 'artisan hotelier', founder of the MOB Hotel and House, two hotels of a new order installed in Saint-Ouen close to the Puces. The former philosophy professor is dedicated to reinventing the hotel industry through initiating new relationships with the living and the non-living. 'The Puces is at once a place and a whole world, a *lieu-monde* that you can visit without taking a plane. It is an example of what our ancestors put in place 150 years ago, which was not at all to save the planet, but which somehow ties in with the question of the protection of the living. These men and women said to themselves, "There's no point in throwing this away, we're going to fix it, transform it," and this is something very close to our mission at MOB, of social ecology. What is ecology, what is a revolution? These are big questions. I think ecology is about doing things. We cannot disconnect the planet from people. We're not saying that we are saving the planet, but we are saying that we are trying to work on the question of the "social artisan", which is to say, putting people who are here in France to work.'

Traditional Craftsmanship — A corner of the Cornu 1887 workshop in Aulnay-sous-Bois. Cornu 1887 is an historic French transport and packing company that works regularly with dealers at the Puces, but also many collectors, galleries and museums around the world, creating custom crates for the transportation of exceptional and rare artworks and furniture, etc. The history of this specialist trade goes back to the sixteenth century, to the *layetier-emballeur*, or box-makers and packers, that took care of the transportation of the personal effects of the French monarchy and nobles, as they moved from castle to castle.

Sidekick — 'My collaborator Arthur Leger, a jack of all trades. He's really smart, he has amazing initiatives, he's sold so much stuff for me. On the weekends when he was minding the stand, he would often call me up, and, if it was a woman that was interested in something, he would say, "Hi Max, I've got this really beautiful woman from America, or Spain, and we were wondering what the best price on something was." And I would tell him the price and five minutes later, he would text me saying it sold. It worked so well. Though unfortunately, my goal of learning French kind of went out the window when he came on board.'

Interior Decoration —

'The lamp on the left is solid bronze, it's Brutalist, from the 60s, the best lamp I've ever found, with the original stitched parchment shade. It came from Germany. I have absolutely no idea who made it, but it's one of my favourite pieces that I've found in a long, long time. I won't be selling it. The coffee table is in the manner of Diego Giacometti. I have no idea who made the pair of green chairs, but I like the feet, they look like sleds, they look quite fun. The iron bell is by Paolo Soleri, an Italian-American architect, probably 1960s. I'm a longtime fan of this artist and I was incredibly lucky to purchase the bell from a dealer in London. Soleri did some crazy, crazy buildings, predominantly architectural work, and then he did other stuff, sculpture, on the side, really beautiful objects.'

Eclectic selection of antiques and art;
all styles and periods

EVA STEINITZ

Modern Design – 'This is the Thonet coat rack, model N°10806, with eight coat hooks and a flap door serving as a dresser caddy supporting an umbrella stand, and with a bevelled mirror at head height. Thonet stamp under the flap. Circa 1900. This object incarnates a point in time when furniture was revolutionized by the Thonet family, the classic German-Viennese cabinetmakers. In 1830, Michael Thonet developed a technique for bending wood. The company quickly sought to patent his invention, which he perfected in the 1850s. Wooden furniture, which previously was necessarily stiff, henceforth became rounder and more flexible, both light and resistant. A revolution! This coat rack is very modern as it does not have to be fixed to a wall since it stands on six feet. It is a very chic object and at the same time fits anywhere. It has a huge personality.'

Romantic Style – 'All the romanticism of the eighteenth century is in these carved wooden angels from Italy, whose polychromy can be detected under the ancient patina. Standing on heaps of gold and silver stones, the movement of the bodies is remarkable; the two statues face each other as if in an embrace. Their expressions are so subtle. Transformed into stands later, they are works of great elegance with obvious charm. Poetic and decorative, I imagine them within a modernist decor, the contrast reinforcing all aspects.'

Eva Steinitz

What does *chiner* mean?

It means to open your eyes, to believe in the beauty of the world, to look in the neighbours' rubbish bins, to not rely on the surface of things, to believe in stories. So-and-so lived in a castle; he had an affair with his maid, who died alone in a cabin in the middle of a forest; a peasant passes by there six generations later, his sheep loses its temper and unearths the buried treasure of the servant of the last king of France …

Are you more tradition or revolution?

I'm a big mix. Life, the mess, the classic and the modern, the tradition of craftsmanship and contemporary action. In art, I obviously like what made a mark in its time, broke codes, jostled genres, but I like the 'followers' too. I love minds that communicate, shared intelligences, 'was influenced by …', Art Deco, Art Nouveau. I think I have a particular weakness for transitions – geographical ones for that matter, I like ports of call, borders and, historically, I love everything around 1900 for example, this mixture of insolence, of travel and the pursuit of stories …

Your biggest influence?

Although it was only over a short time in reality, the influence of my father is indisputable. That I broke out on my own I think has a lot to do with him. Because he trusted me and supported me with my desire for individuality very early. And he affirmed his own sense of taste too, never hesitating (even when it was not yet fashionable) to take risks by mixing styles and eras. It was with him, as a child, that I discovered the professional markets at dawn, the hunt for beauty with a flashlight … My father would have accepted anything I did professionally, but he cannot know (he died when I was 20), that like him, I trace my path revolving around my artistic disposition.

Your greatest extravagance?

To believe in myself. I believe in myself while having a very small ego. Certainly I think I'm capable of finding interesting, beautiful things in the middle of all the crap of the universe. But for all that, I have a penchant for bad taste, for what is not fashionable, what resembles vulgarity, etc. It amuses me and depresses me to try to have 'good taste', I don't like the feeling of superiority. I don't want to be obsessed with pleasing, with corresponding either to fashion, the diktats of the market, or to an idea of beauty; I prefer charm, to speak to muted sensitivities, and arouse curiosities, ways of seeing that are not predictable.

Your favourite tool?

My eye. To get the courage to start out, trusting my eye was what took the longest. It's terribly exciting to trust it so completely, it's very creative too. I had a creative bent when I was younger, and I am enormously fulfilled in this sense as a dealer today.

How did you get where you are?

On my maternal side, there is also a history of art dealers. My grandfather Sylvain Chamak, an Algerian Jew from a family of 20 children, was a second-hand dealer at the Puces. It is important for me to mark the link between the gallery of Faubourg-St-Honoré of my paternal grandfather Bernard Steinitz, and the piled-on-the-footpath flea market of the Puces on my maternal side. Europe and Africa … I recognize myself enormously in this link, this bridge.

What has, or hasn't, changed at the Puces?

There is the school of 'it was better before'. I hear of those Friday mornings when the goods were snatched up by dealers 'from the back of the truck'. It seems that business was easier, the goods more accessible; I didn't know this time, but I really enjoy the legend. But I'm not nostalgic at all. The Puces, in my opinion, will always remain the world's greatest antiques warehouse.

Does the Puces make the world a better place?

Art makes the world better, it allows us to survive depressions, both universal and personal, it allows us to understand the world differently, and to open up to other perspectives and visions.

What can you only find at the Puces?

There is a form of anonymity in which everyone is equal.

Favourite time of day?

I love to set up. My stand is very small, and each day expresses my state of mind, which I will accentuate if it is cheerful or soften if it is melancholy. Very early on I exuberantly arranged pieces outside my stand. For a while now I have had a beautiful Turkish kilim from the 70s on which I stage each week's show. Some days, my installation is very quick, I hurry to go and drink a coffee with my friends; other mornings I hang around and move an object at the back of the stand a millimetre to the left then a millimetre to the right a thousand times … This is the poetics of presentation.

Do you have to be a bit crazy to work at the Puces?

We live out of step with the whole of society. When other people are walking in the forest, having lunch with their family, going to the movies or spending lazy mornings, we are playing out our 'destiny'. This motivates me to have the best possible time on site. Thus, eccentricities are welcome, ideas for having a good time without moving are invented. In the alleys of the Puces, you find the aesthetic outsiders, those who have become over the years a masterpiece of self-creation; the altruists, who organize large tables to welcome neighbours and visitors throughout the day; or those who create a universe in which they manage to feel elsewhere … All this to somehow counterbalance the ingratitude of not being able to enjoy the weekends like the majority of people, which actually makes us a little crazy.

Do you have a motto?

I have many mantras that guide me … 'The best is the enemy of the good.' This means that you have to know when to stop, to get out of the game at the right time. It's a very useful motto in auctions. And 'to make your life a work of art' … by Picasso I believe?

Eva Steinitz

Sentimental Value – 'As the daughter and granddaughter of dealers, I live with pieces that I have known for a long time, like this dressing table that has been with me since I was 12. I love dressing tables. I'm not sure if it was actually mine at the time, or just in the apartment where we lived and where furniture would often disappear overnight. I appropriated it, but today it's no longer totally to my taste. It is an Empire style mahogany dressing table with a white veined marble top and an eagle's head on each side of the mirror. There is also a gorgeous fish head on either side of the foot. It's an object that, let's say, I'm stuck with, that follows me, that I have permeated. I am very fetishistic. I attach importance to scraps of paper left by my children, things that remind me of a past moment, a person; I keep sand from my travels, pebbles, stones, shells; I dry herbs; I keep obsolete objects to remind me of the people I loved who are no longer here. I keep clothes so damaged that they cannot be worn, broken things ... I have a very sentimental relationship with things, with objects, and it's the same on my stand.'

Wow Factor – 'This piece radiates a feeling of transparency and voluptuousness, playing with the light that it absorbs and reflects. The pink backlighting on the sides of the console amplify it with a halo of glamour. The icing on the cake is that the material is recyclable. Produced by DBM Mobili, a Tuscan furniture company dating back to the early 1900s, it is an exceptional piece, whose curved design recalls the Art Deco period. In lacquered wood, Altuglas and black plexiglass veined like marble, the materials evoke the future. Altuglas acrylic resin appeared in design at the beginning of the 1960s, and became de rigueur in the 70s, when creativity was limitless. This dressing table embodies everything I love, it creates a décor all on its own.'

Hot Desk — 'A rare desk by Louis Paolozzi, made in the 1950s. The two-drawer unit opens in front, and the top, in blond oak, sits on a base enhanced with a shelf. It's an extraordinary design, beautiful from all sides, and with ideal dimensions. Often associated with the post-war reconstruction period, Louis Paolozzi distinguished himself by producing furniture with flexible shapes, playing on the recesses and broken lines that reference Italian production of the era. In collaboration with furniture companies such as René Godfrid, as for this desk, the designer developed a style that is both graphic and functional, enhanced by a pronounced attention to detail.'

Behind the Scenes – A detail of a sales room at the Hôtel Drouot auction house. 'I lived the first thirteen years of my life at 4 rue Drouot. The auction house, opposite, embodied an extension to our apartment. Today I visit Drouot every day, meticulously, in detail, returning constantly. I search and dissect everything that piques my curiosity. There are a thousand ways to do this job. Ninety-nine per cent of the time, I buy at auctions and almost exclusively online (I like being anonymous behind my screen). Today we have access to almost every auction in France, and increasingly throughout Europe, it's dizzying. From modest, common sales to the richest catalogues, treasure is everywhere.'

Family Affair – Inside the Galerie Steinitz at 6 Rue Royale in Paris. 'My grandfather Bernard Steinitz began his professional activity in 1968. I believe that success only came to him in the early 80s. He had five children including my father David, the eldest – whom he had at just 20 years old, in a period of epic economic struggles, so far from what we recollect today. Followed by Mireille, Paul, Benjamin, and Sarah. Today, Benjamin is the great antique dealer of the family. He has managed to combine respect for family history with revolution. Working alongside him for a while taught me a lot. Benjamin has plenty of wit and humour, I think you can detect his intelligence within his displays and it's very inspiring. I took some time to find my path in life, but in the end the apple didn't fall far from the tree.'

Eva Steinitz

The Secret Life of the Puces — 'There is an unimaginable ecosystem within the Puces. We work surrounded by a thousand different small tradespeople who make our lives easier. We are happy to coexist with them through objects. Mike, who transports all the furniture within the Puces with his cart; Kasha, who takes care of all the odd jobs on our stands; Bidou, who transports sales to our customers in Paris and its suburbs, even to a sixth-floor walk-up; Rahba who goes beyond the Paris region, for the same impeccable service ... But also Afida, who, like a saint, brings us mint tea every day between 4 and 5 p.m., allowing us to warm our hands in winter; Péra and his magnificent flowers; and Marc or Daniel who fix the electricity of the oldest or most dilapidated lights.'

100 OBJETS ANCIENS

Marché Paul Bert
Allée 3, Stand 48
@bernard_tinivella

Roman sculpture, neoclassical, Grand Tour

BERNARD TINIVELLA

Modern-day Michelangelo — 'This statue is a copy of Michelangelo's *David*, from the beginning of the twentieth century. It adorned a villa in Cannes, on the French Riviera and it was assaulted, broken — we can see shovel blows. It's a shame, because it's well made, it's a beautiful piece of real white Carrara, it costs a lot of money to get a block like that. The person who made it was a good artist, it's a fine copy of the Michelangelo.'

Bernard Tinivella

Sacred Goddess – 'I think this must be Venus, it is a work that is not of a particularly high quality of execution, but it is full of charm. It is from before the Common Era, but Roman. I find it moving, because certainly the person who made it was not a great artist, but he wanted to represent beauty, and above all the goddess. Because we must not forget, statues had a function of representation and worship too, they allowed people to pray or reflect, just like the Christian effigies that we see, of the different saints that people adored. There is something sacred in it and it is this aspect that interests me.'

What is your expertise, speciality or particularity?
Ancient Rome, and the neoclassical more generally. Neoclassical is everything from the end of the eighteenth, beginning of the nineteenth century. At the end of the eighteenth century came the Enlightenment, Voltaire, Rousseau, which pushed the world forward, as it emerged from the shackles of religion – this is very important. Before, the writings of Plato and Socrates were forbidden by the Church. People were now able to access knowledge of the ancient world, with the discovery of Pompei, Napoleon Bonaparte and Egypt, the deciphering of hieroglyphs by Champollion … all of this contributed to the arts, to culture, to everything. This made people look at the ancient world with a new eye, and it became fashionable for the nobility, especially the English, to undertake the Grand Tour, to visit Paris, Venice, Florence, and above all Rome, as the culmination of their education. All gentlemen had to know the wonders of the world. They took an interest in ancient sculpture and copied everything they saw, which allowed them to have the whole ancient world at home.

Why the Puces?
I used to come here when I was 17, to buy my jazz records and wander around. I was a bit of a musician myself, my father was a conductor, he played in a jazz orchestra. All my life I have been nurtured by the great American jazz standards: Stan Getz, Duke Ellington, Charlie Parker, the greatest, Coltrane. Throughout my early childhood my father would come into the kitchen and play, and I liked to listen under the kitchen table, it made me dream, just like the gaze of the statues of Apollo, or listening to Mozart. Listening to my dad playing the great standards of Stan Getz forged my vision of the world.

What has, or hasn't, changed at the Puces?
Once a den of crooks, scoundrels, colourful characters, today watered down and ordinary.

Do you have to be a bit crazy to work at the Puces?
Yes, it's a profession for social outcasts.

Does the Puces de Saint Ouen have a sister elsewhere on the planet?
Portobello Market in London, and the Città Antiquaria Fossano in Italy, which looks surprisingly like the Marché Serpette.

How did you get where you are?
I was born in Algeria, to an Italian family who arrived in 1870, who participated in the French conquest of Algeria, with Bugeaud, Cavaignac. When they arrived they were given land, and they settled in the Sétif region, the Constantinois, where on the coast are marvellous sites such as Tipaza and Cherchell. The Romans always chose the most beautiful sites to settle, and the Greeks too, there is always beauty, something fantastic, in the places they chose. I have wonderful memories of going for picnics by the sea with my uncle, then playing in the ruins.

Who are you?
Always out of step.

Describe your stand.
A pile of useless objects, but oh, how dear to my heart. There is an osmosis between the pieces; they are me, I am them, there is a symbiosis. I feel as though I am in a cocoon, like in the matrix, for me that's it, it's my world. Here I sit, listening to music, I can dream.

What inspires you?
One can be moved by small, banal things. The things that affect you may not be of great value materially, but have great spiritual value. I am an antique dealer, I must earn my living, but that's not what interests me, at all, it's not about the money, I don't care. When I fall in love with an object, it represents many things for me; I see through the object to the person who made it, the material used, the work, the finish, all that it had to undergo to reach us, that's what interests me. It connects me to the ancient world.

Is there an element of magic to your work?
Of course. The beautiful, the extraordinary. It's a wonderful world, even if only to own an object that once belonged to someone in the seventeenth or eighteenth century, or in Roman times. Someone was able to contemplate a statue of Apollo, and now I am looking at it. For me, it's a miracle! All these generations who preceded us and who gave us the best of themselves, that which remains touches me deeply.

Your favourite tool?
My experienced eye.

Do you buy to sell, or sell to buy?
I'm a compulsive buyer, completely insane. An object pleases me, I want to own it because I find it so beautiful, so magnificent, it speaks to me. I buy stuff for the pleasure of buying it, and then I don't know what to do with it. I already have so much at home, I had to take this stand especially to put everything in. But I can't help it, all this accumulation, it's me, it's my life. I like it, it's silly I know.

Essential artisan or craft for you?
It's very complicated, because a restorer must also be someone who has a sensitivity, who can understand the object, by looking at it, by restoring it to its true initial shape, and it's very difficult, sometimes we are terribly disappointed. There are very few marble restorers, it's a disappearing art.

What do you do when you are not working?
I listen to Baroque music. It's a huge part of my life. All the great musicians, Henry Purcell, Handel, Bach, of course, and Mozart, who has been my favourite for a very long time, and Beethoven; all these extraordinary people, who are inspired by God, to write such works. I feel touched, as if by grace; it's part of what is beautiful in the world, and I take full advantage of it.

Does the Puces make the world a better place?
The world counterbalances it.

If you weren't at the Puces, where would you be?
In an urn, in the cemetery.

Bernard Tinivella

124

Ancient Relic –
A contemporary portrait of Louis XIV from 1689, wearing a Roman cuirass and cloak, by Antoine Coysevox in the Cour d'Honneur of the Musée Carnavalet, Paris. 'The great century of Louis XIV saw the emergence of a new world, of this modern new king, who wanted to put France at the heart of Europe, at the heart of the world. He was undoubtedly a megalomaniac, but with hindsight, everything he managed to do was beneficial for our kingdom of France. In the arts, he knew how to develop all that was most beautiful; it was to his glory, but it still serves us today. He was one of the greatest collectors of his time. A great copier of the Greek and Roman worlds. Louis XIV had extraordinary collections of ancient relics that he copied for his gardens, for his palaces, all kinds of things. He was an incredible disseminator, in the seventeenth and eighteenth centuries, of this craze for the ancient arts.'

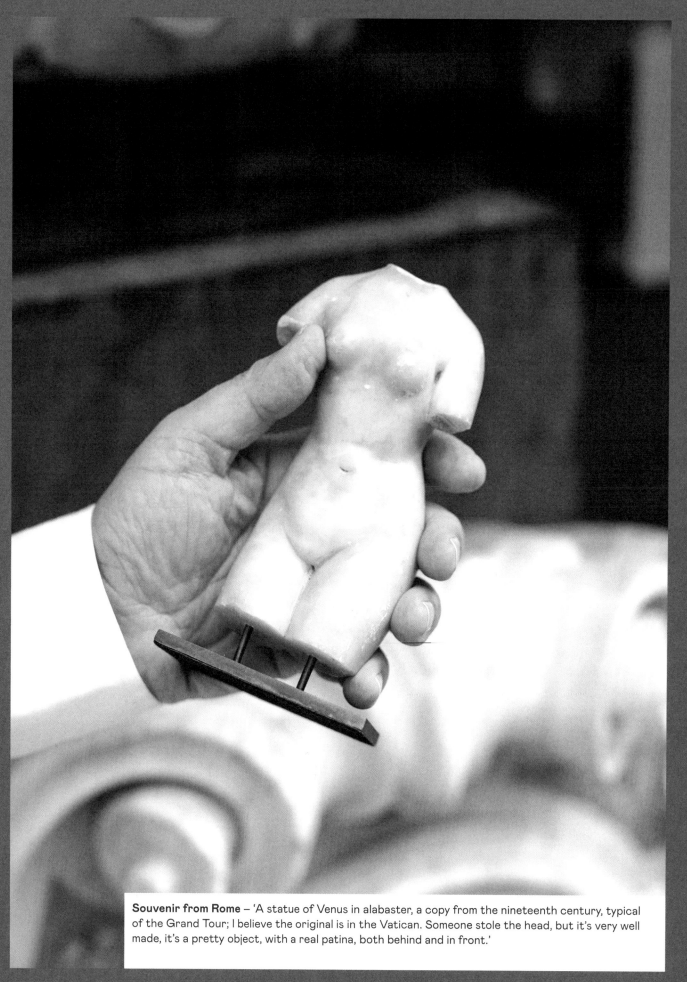

Souvenir from Rome – 'A statue of Venus in alabaster, a copy from the nineteenth century, typical of the Grand Tour; I believe the original is in the Vatican. Someone stole the head, but it's very well made, it's a pretty object, with a real patina, both behind and in front.'

Essential Reading – 'The *Odyssey*, the story of Ulysses, is one of the greatest books of antiquity, along with Virgil's epic poem about the Trojan war, the *Aeneid*. These are my favourite books. As a child, reading the *Odyssey* made me dream, catapulting me amongst Achilles and all his great Greek heroes. History has inspired me all my life; the ancient world, Egyptian as well as Greek and Roman. I am an ardent fan.'

VIRGILE
ÉNÉIDE

Homère
Iliade – Odyssée

The Ancient World – 'A Roman bust in Carrara marble, from the first or second century, certainly a great dignitary, a senator or an emperor, who was sculpted wearing a chlamys, a sort of cloak, very common at the time. The drapery is rendered beautifully. The head was, like all heads, broken, so only the torso remains. Heads are the easiest to break, and let's not forget that the first Christians, when they were able to establish their religion, took revenge on all these effigies of god, these idols, and broke their noses, or their heads.'

Best Find – 'A Roman sarcophagus, first to third century AD, the third I've found, and likely to be the last. The lion's feet are seventeenth century, but I find that it gives the sarcophagus more allure; normally it would have been placed on a platform. Engraved on the façade, a winged female figure sings the praises of the deceased. Sarcophagi were only for the extremely rich – a Carrara marble sarchophagus cost a fortune, and you had to have a certain rank to even have the right to have one, and then somewhere to put it as well. More modest people had a simple urn for their ashes, sealed with lead. The two on the columns flanking the sarcophagus are made of Comblanchien limestone. They are two thousand years old but have an extraordinarily modern aspect. We didn't invent anything, the ancients had already invented everything before us, then it was taken up, copied.'

BENOÎT ASTIER DE VILLATTE & IVAN PERICOLI

Designers
Astier de Villatte
www.astierdevillatte.com

Ivan: 'For us, the Puces is above all a kind of urban utopia. It's an anachronism, a space that doesn't exist anywhere else. There are flea markets all over the world, but there's nothing like this in the world; it's a kind of folly.

We often say that Astier de Villatte is a character in perpetual psychoanalysis. He experienced a trauma linked to modernity – a bit like Jason Bourne, he got hit on the head and doesn't know who he is any more, so he tries to make up his own past. And it's by going to the Puces that this character of Astier de Villatte manages to do that.'

Benoît: 'In a sense, Ivan and I were kind of brought up by our painting teacher at the Beaux-Arts in Paris, Georges Jeanclos. Our generation was opposed to the Puces, to that idea, the idea of old things. There was modernity, abstraction; figuration was dead! All that was a discourse that was extremely strong until the 90s. But parallel to that, there were people like our teacher, who had decided to settle in the countryside, who only bought old things because he felt that beauty was not necessarily something modern. In modernity there is a form of vanity, of the entire era, that wants to believe that it will do better, in all areas, than previous eras. But these people said no, not at all; we sit on fertile soil, which is the soil of history, and here we build something. The Puces is part of this soil, along with museums. There's not much difference between a museum and the Puces.'

Ivan: 'The Puces is both a direct and indirect source of inspiration for us. Often, to make a new dish, a new plate, we take a piece of something that we reinterpret, that we transform. We always start from something that exists, and of course it might come from the market. But beyond that, it's an atmosphere, a place of freedom, of creativity. The air that blows through Paris inspires us, and I find that the Puces is the most Parisian thing there is. Paris is changing a lot, gentrifying, but the Puces not so much; it retains a bit of the spirit of freedom that Paris once had.'

Benoît Astier de Villatte and Ivan Pericoli photographed at the Astier de Villatte headquarters in Paris, in Benoît's office.

Galerie Vauclair
Marché Paul Bert, Allée 6, Stand 79
and Paris: 24 rue de Beaune, 75007
@galerievauclair
galerie-vauclair.fr

Rattan furniture and ceramics from
the second half of the nineteenth century;
Barbotine, Majolica, Palissy, Massier, Deck,
Lachenal, Minton

LAURENCE VAUCLAIR & DENIS ROUQUETTE

Why the Puces?

L: There's nothing like it anywhere else in the world. It's impossible to ignore when you are an antique dealer in Paris. It is the heart of the antiques world, whether for the second-hand *brocante* (and for me the word *brocante* is not pejorative) at the Jules Vallès and Vernaison markets; for innovation in trends with the influencers of Paul Bert; for the trendy and jet-setter side of Serpette. There's also the Biron market, with its lavish Arabian Nights decor, its tassels and gilded bronze. The Puces is like trying to make fire with a piece of wood and a flint, everything rubs up against everything else, and the reactions are unpredictable.

How did you get where you are?

L: My parents loved browsing second-hand shops and markets, and always took me to museums too. My mum was a hairdresser and my father was an important tailor who dressed General de Gaulle, and who made the uniforms for the members of the Académie Française. So I grew up surrounded by fabrics, luxury, embroidery. Inevitably, my eye has been educated since I was little. I loved browsing old things with my parents. One day a woman opened a second-hand shop opposite my mother's shop and we became friends. She introduced me to people including to a woman who participated in all the Foire de Chatou antiques fairs. I got involved through her. I started buying pieces and selling at small fairs to make some money on weekends. I met dealers from all over France. You buy, you sell, you make mistakes, but you always have pieces in your hands. There was no internet then so you went to the school of life, you went to museums and you read, that's it. You learned by yourself, by experience and through others.

Your favourite tool?

L: Instagram, which gives the whole world access to our work.

Tell us about your stand.

L: I'm lucky to have a large boutique at the Puces that has a big window, so it really looks like a shop. I'm also lucky to have my stockrooms next door; I restore, I repair, I stock in Saint-Ouen. This stand was built after the war by Jews returning from the camps. Paul Bert was a vacant lot where plots of land were given to dispossessed Jews. They built shacks there, which is why the Paul Bert market has the particularity of being made up of small shacks that are all different. My stand belonged to Polish Jews: the Apelstein family, who were my neighbours for ten years. They built it with their own hands.

Essential artisan or craft for you?

L: Between the artist and the craftsman there is but a small step, and craft is essential for preserving the value and the techniques of our heritage. We all work closely together, like a very solid chain in which none of the links must be missing.

What is a typical day for you?

L: It starts with a coffee at my friend Sylvie Lacombe's café, La Chope des Puces. Then I drop my stuff at my stand and go for a stroll around the surrounding markets, Paul Bert and Jules Vallès. Next, I open my shop. I install the rattan furniture and flowers outside, then I open my laptop and check my emails. I already checked the social networks much earlier. Throughout the morning, we greet and chat a lot with different dealers. Around 2 p.m., I have lunch on my stand. I always order from La Péricole, a restaurant that I particularly like. The afternoon is spent welcoming clients, dealers and collectors. I usually finish at 6 or 6.30 p.m. From time to time we have a drink in the evening, at La Chope des Puces or at the MOB Hotel.

What has, or hasn't, changed at the Puces?

L: The reputation of the Puces has changed, perhaps with the arrival of more bling-bling, more prominent dealers. Perhaps also with 'younger' merchandise, with dealers now who specialize in the 50s and 60s, 70s and 80s, 90s and 2000s, which has attracted a different clientele, without driving away the others. There are fewer eighteenth-century goods than before. Before, you didn't say you had a stand at the Puces when you had a shop in the Carré Saint-Germain. We had two business cards and we didn't mix the two. But the Puces has become the place to be, everyone comes here. It has become very fashionable, very high-profile. The dealers who made the Puces are still the same though. We've always had a lot of celebrities, the biggest ones have always shopped here. All the decorators are here. The atmosphere is crazy. Saint-Ouen is also trying to fit into a new dynamic.

Does research and documentation take up a lot of your time?

L: Of course. To shed light on all the immense artists forgotten through the passage of time, it is crucial to trace their legacies, studios and creations. The close handling of objects has sharpened my eye over the years, and I want to share these treasures. In 2002, I became a member of the Chambre National des Experts Specialisés (CNES) and the Syndicat National des Antiquaires (SNA), becoming an official expert in Majolica and artistic ceramics. I carry out research and take on documentation assistants, always from the École du Louvre. We really bought these ceramics back into fashion – the Palissy style, the Massiers – by explaining the grandeur of this period, and of the Expositions Universelles. We built this ceramic style's popularity, and market value. Everything was up for grabs back then, it was a real niche.

What is luxury?

L: Knowing how to surround yourself with interesting people.

Is there an element of magic to your work?

L: My profession is magic and my husband is a magician. I am Alice in Wonderland and he is the Wizard of Oz.

Laurence Vauclair & Denis Rouquette

For Sale — 'This bamboo showcase with baluster and shelf, circa 1880, is by the Parisian manufacturer Perret & Vibert and testifies to the growing Asian influence in the decorative arts of the time. The interior in embossed and gilded paper imitating Cordoba leather, combined with the speckled varnish on the bamboo, manifests a taste for the grandiose so characteristic of nineteenth-century winter gardens. These new domestic spaces were extensions of the living and dining rooms: reception rooms imbued with a leisurely and luxuriant atmosphere inspired by nature.'

Best Find – 'About fifteen years ago, I bought this piece, which intrigued me a lot, because it has a very bizarre signature, and an unusual decor. It looks like a Théodore Deck, but it's signed Doré. It's the Deck blue, but its shape doesn't exist in the Deck repertoire, and it's unsigned by him. We did a lot of research, for a long time. We consulted an expert to test the clay, glaze, and pigments, and to try to identify the potter and the engraver. What also piqued our curiosity was Doré's double signature, since obviously Gustave Doré didn't make ceramics. Then we found a report from 1862 in which it's noted that Gustave Doré and Théodore Deck planned to make a piece of great importance! Could ours be a study for this monumental piece? Obviously, I want it to be Doré because it would be worth millions of euros. But for now, we don't know where this piece comes from ... This is what's so interesting about my profession.'

Laurence Vauclair & Denis Rouquette

158

Majolica Mania – 'In 2021 I did an exhibition dedicated to Linda Horn and her book *Majolica Mania*, which included this piece, a heron and pike ewer modelled by Hugues Protât for Minton, 1867. Meeting Linda Horn is the reason I made the switch to Majolica ware. Linda is one of the greatest decorators in the United States, and the greatest collector of Majolica. I met her in 1998, at the Miami Beach Antique Show and she became my mentor. I went with my Meissen and French porcelain; I knew nothing then about Majolica and rattan, winter gardens and Palissy Ware. It looked slimy next to my Meissen porcelain, which is so fragile and so pretty, but that's all everyone wanted. All my life I'll remember saying to myself, "How ugly!" But I started buying these kinds of pieces, and I returned to Miami the following year.'

Laurence Vauclair & Denis Rouquette

The Crystal Palace – 'English Majolica, originated by Minton, was first exhibited at the very first Exposition Universelle, which took place in London in 1851, and the French quickly followed. My favourite historical period is 1850–1900, the period of the Expositions Universelles. These fairs were really the opening of a door to creativity, and so to extraordinary freedom, and beauty. All these artists, whether ceramicists, jewellers, craftsmen who worked bronze or wood … converged here, and the first meeting was in 1851, in a place that is completely crazy, the Crystal Palace. It was the beginning of a new era. It's something that still dazzles me. We think that we are free, but there was a spirit of cultural freedom then that makes us look poor today.'

Salon Style – 'This is a pretty little Parisian winter garden in Paris belonging to one of our customers, and decorated with pieces from the gallery. A winter garden or conservatory is a room that you create adjoining the house, where you can be outside while being inside, and have tea and receive people, and have salon discussions. They are fanciful spaces. They became fashionable in the nineteenth century. If you google the painting by Sébastien-Charles Giraud, *La Véranda de la Princesse Mathilde*, you see it's the extension of her living room, and you have a huge glass roof and fabrics and tapestries, ceramics, pot plants, a bit like here.'

Gypsy Jazz – Portrait of jazz manouche swing guitarist Simone Magliozzi outside La Chope des Puces. 'My day begins with a coffee at my friend Sylvie's café La Chope des Puces, which is also the last place I go, for a drink while listening to jazz manouche. This is where jazz manouche was born, the descendants of Django Reinhardt still come here. It's really something very special, and is a refuge sometimes for me from the madness of the Puces.'

Garden Furniture – 'Natural rattan armchair, circa 1880, Perret & Vibert. The natural honey colour of the rattan as well as its elaborate weaving make it a piece that is both welcoming and decorative. Its finesse demonstrates the excellence achieved by Parisian artisans, who created modern rattan furniture that was ever lighter and more decorative. The exoticism in fashion during the Second Empire explains the craze for this furniture which took off with the massive importation of raw materials from China and Indochina. It is in this context that the major Parisian houses developed. Perret & Vibert, later known as the "Maison des Bambous", opened in 1872 in Paris, and presented its creations at numerous Expositions Universelles, even taking home two silver medals in 1889.'

Laurence Vauclair & Denis Rouquette

Turning Point – 'Meeting Leila Menchari, Hermès' legendary window dresser, changed my life. Hermès to me was like the moon. One day Mlle Menchari walked into my boutique in Paris – she lived on the same street – and we started talking; she stayed for more than three hours. She went on to buy or borrow a large number of my pieces, including this pair of Choisy-le-Roi ceramic elephant planters, circa 1880, to decorate all eleven windows of Hermès Rue du Faubourg Saint-Honoré. This had never happened to an antique dealer before. We were invited to the inauguration of the windows, for autumn 2011, and her kindness and decency extended to crediting each piece Galerie Vauclair. There was a before and an after.'

Laurence Vauclair & Denis Rouquette

Museum Piece – 'This ewer in the shape of a wolf's head by Charles-Joseph Landais was acquired by the Musée des Arts Décoratifs in 2012. It's the most beautiful piece by Landais that they have, and a really major piece of Palissy Ware. The wolf, typically associated with fear, with darkness, is a motif that we've never, ever seen in Palissy Ware. We are proud that the museum acquired it, that they recognize our work and our intuition, and that we discovered something so rare and unusual. But above all we are happy that many people will see it, that we can contribute in a small way to history.'

Marché Serpette
Allée 6, Stands 4&5

Galerie Martel Greiner
71 boulevard Raspail
75006 Paris
@hgdesigngallery

Modern sculpture, Surrealist painting,
and twentieth-century furniture,
particularly American

HUGO GREINER

Abstract Sculpture – 'Louis Thomas-d'Hoste is a French sculptor who was part of the New School of Paris, which was kind of like the last Modernist surge in art, essentially represented in sculpture. It was the breeding ground for the generation of César, Cárdenas, and all those artists. What I really like about this piece, *Cosmogonie*, is this idea, with the white veining in the black marble, of representing the subject within the material. It also represents an aspect of sculpture which is of great interest to the gallery, the work of direct carving, a type of sculpture that is not necessarily the most visible — we hear more about the modellers and those who make bronzes.'

Why the Puces?

It's my home, my life, my family, as are art galleries. Both my parents had a career here, antique dealer for my mother and *brocanteur* for my father. The Puces is a bit like my bedroom. At six years old I was reading *Tintin* and *Asterix* stashed between two dressers upstairs in Allée 6 of the Paul Bert market. At 15, I earned pocket money by helping my parents or by watching a stand. At 20 I was earning my stripes, and today, past 30, I'm still here.

Tell us about your stand.

Since 2010, I have forged my specialities. I am passionate about so many movements and artists that it has not always been easy for me to be limited, like many, to three names or one style. I am eclectic, but my stand presents of course very specialized aspects: Surrealism and abstract art in painting, historical Modern sculpture from 1920 to 1980, and American and iconic European furniture are my bases. I am also a great lover of Italian and Finnish glassware, and rare light fixtures.

Is there an image from the past that obsesses or inspires you?

I am passionate about Surrealism, and op and abstract art; the 60s enthusiasm for scientific discoveries, psychedelia and futurism inspires me a lot. The music of the time was also illustrated by Art Nouveau style graphics: Grateful Dead or Quicksilver Messenger Service covers.

Your best find?

There have been several, but a piece now sold that I'd like to share is a terracotta pitcher by Maurice Savin, a great artist from the South of France from the early twentieth century, a naive painter and decorator. Representing the neoclassical theme of Leda and the Swan, this piece was presented in 1933 at the Petit Palais for a retrospective of the artist. It is a museum piece, despite its modest dimensions. You can be a recognized dealer in design and decorative arts and be interested in this kind of piece.

An unforgettable piece or sale?

A Sonia Delaunay rug sold to Karl Lagerfeld himself.

What does *chiner* mean?

Chiner is to be attentive to everything, to sense things without thinking too much in the moment, because reflection is permanent, really. To constantly gain knowledge and to move around is advantageous. You need your playing field, but not to get too stuck in it, and ignore the opinions of others. When you make a mistake, you pay for it and you learn. But you have to have looked at a lot of things first, and trust your intuition, even when you are mocked. It's not as simple as people think, above all we're not buying for ourselves, it's not shopping.

What's your motto?

'*Comparaison n'est pas raison*' [comparison is not reason]. I apply it in the sense that you have to do what you know, what you like, and improve and not let yourself be too seduced by the desire to imitate other people, thinking that you will have the same success. The priority is to become autonomous in relation to your tastes, your knowledge, and your expertise. It can be tempting to abandon these priorities for something that seems to work better for others, when often it's just a question of time and persistence. This job is really about creating an enduring dialogue with buyers, and this dialogue is your credibility. I work quite a bit with collectors, more than auction houses.

Is the Puces only the tip of the iceberg?

The Puces is more like a mountain, and the market is the ground water; everything is connected.

Your favourite period, movement, or style?

Late nineteenth century English, Italian and German (personal taste and former activity), French and Dutch Modernism.

Does the Puces make the world a better place?

The Puces can serve to preserve the memory of human creation, to understand where we come from. And the interest for the past, in the present, obviously serves for the future.

Where does your inspiration come from?

Music. I'm a guitarist, and passionate about string instruments, banjo, mandolin. Music gives me the rhythm to create ensembles, and rock, cumbia, country, blues are my oxygen. Without this passion I would be nothing.

A favourite book, film, song, or other work?

Scheherazade by Nikolai Rimsky-Korsakov, and *Farenheit 451* by François Truffaut. There are many others.

Who is your hero?

Nikola Tesla and Rory Gallagher. I have a weakness for misunderstood geniuses.

Have the internet and social networks changed the way you work?

Yes, especially for auctions, which I no longer like because of the traceability and the false objectivity they promise; it's the same for Google, not everything is there, at all, but the public thinks the opposite. The eye, books, and a good memory, are worth all the search engines.

Are you more tradition or revolution?

Tradition of the revolution. We're in France after all. But without being too clever, for me the old and the new are much more connected than one can see or believe. In fact, a rupture does not even exist.

I have a time machine; where do we go?

To Berlin in 1896, it was a hotbed for artists. Or 1968, along the Californian coast.

Your biggest extravagance?

There are many. Apparently, I often appear slightly mad.

Do you have to be a bit crazy to work at the Puces?

You have to be crazy to be a dealer, but with enough sense to not go completely nuts. It's an occupational hazard, and waiting two days for a miracle can drive you crazy too.

Is there an element of magic to your work?

Yes, you never know what's about to happen, especially when nothing has happened for a long time. You start to question yourself, you can feel like a loser, then you can feel like a star for a minute, then a loser again. But we believe in this magic of the impossible moment.

Working from Life – 'A very good artist, of Hungarian origin, François Kovacs attended the School of Fine Arts in Budapest, but studied medicine at the same time. When he settled in Belgium, he had a career as an artist in parallel with his work as a doctor, and in particular, as a researcher. He carried out research using a microscope on bone tissue, which explains his works' organic and scientific nature, which he manages to express with unparalleled marble work. What is really interesting about him is that his work really comes from observation, not only invention. This piece is relatively small, but he also worked on a much larger scale; for example, he created several monumental works for the sculpture garden in Jeddah, in Saudi Arabia, alongside greats like Louise Bourgeois and Miró.'

Hugo Greiner

Contemporary Artisan – 'Mathieu Houlbert is one of two contemporary designers that I work with. I've been selling contemporary stuff for a while, but I only sell atelier-produced, one-off pieces. No industrial stuff. Houlbert is a cabinetmaker, a carpenter, a sculptor, he has worked on many very beautiful projects, from designing bicycles to propellers. His personality really stands out in this "Cathedrale" series of chairs.'

Public Art – *Les Sphérades*, kinetic fountain sculpture, Pol Bury, 1985. 'This fountain-sculpture is installed in the Palais Royal, where it interacts with the adjacent Colonnes de Buren. We see it inert, but it's actually a motorized work; the movement of the water flowing over the spheres and the rotation of the sphere reflected in the water give it a whole other dimension. There's this notion of optical art, Surrealist art, something very futuristic, both dreamy and mechanical. My mother represented Pol Bury. He belongs to a generation of artists associated with Vasarely and is known for his work involving spheres; he was very inspired by a large painting by Magritte, *The Voice of Space*.'

Voodoo – 'One of my lucky charms. It's always on my stand. A dealer gave it to me. Giving a mineral to someone is a gesture of good will. It's a copper rock, mineral copper which has oxidized, and which created these sort of copper hematites, between hematite and marcasite, it's quite unusual and quite pretty. I like stones. In the Jardin des Plantes in Paris there is a geology and mineralogy museum with one of the world's most beautiful collections of semi-precious stones and rare minerals.'

Hugo Greiner

Essential Reading – 'My most precious possessions are my musical instruments and my books. In a former concierge's lodge that I took over in Rue de Fleurus I've installed bookshelves where I keep my father's library, my mother's library, and my own collection. Sometimes I have three copies of the same book.'

Hugo Greiner

Left Bank Heritage – 'My mother Hélène Greiner was pregnant with me when she opened the gallery in 1990, the same year as my birth. It was her first gallery, a place where she held many exhibitions, and I decided to take it over after she died in 2021. 71 Boulevard Raspail is located between the historic artists' quarter of Montparnasse, and Saint Germain, which is the historic art gallery quarter. So the gallery is in between the two. Montmartre was associated with Symbolism, but Modern, Expressionist, Post-Impressionist art, and artists like Soutine, Zadkine, and Modigliani, were associated with Montparnasse, what we call the School of Paris.'

GALERIE MARTEL - GREINER

71

Totemism – 'Daniel Ghiatza, 1968, teak and bronze sculpture. It's an intriguing piece. At first glance, it's an African sculpture, with a beautiful direct carving style; in its spirit, features and proportions, it is almost a stereotype. There is a whole message behind the very beautifully made, extremely figurative and realistic bronze snake, which perverts the sculpture's dreamlike dimension, and in my eyes, symbolizes the West. We're in the 60s–70s, with a new reading of what in the past was judged as primitive. New ideas assert themselves, inspired by Claude Lévi-Strauss and the rest.'

Hugo Greiner

156

Op Art – *Vertical-Charbon* by Leopoldo Torres-Agüero, 1971, acrylic on canvas. 'Torres-Agüero is an extremely interesting Argentinian artist who left his mark on the world of op art. He returned from Japan in 1961 influenced by the principles of Satori and Zen, and moved more and more towards the geometric, endeavouring to access truth without artifice. This painting is made from dripping paint down the canvas in a controlled flow. He often painted with his eyes closed to sense the paint flowing, bringing to his work a whole spiritual and symbolic dimension, nourished by his experience in Japan.'

AURÉLIEN SERRE

Dreamscape – 'These "cocoon" lamps by Achille et Pier Castiglioni were first created in the 60s and are more or less rare depending on the model. A few have become iconic, like the Viscontea on the left, which is still produced by Flos today. They are made by spraying polymer resin onto a wire structure – pioneering materials and techniques at the time. The trio of oak tables that look like little clouds are from Holland, and date from the 60s. I don't know the designer, but a piece's graphic quality, its proportions and what it radiates are just as important to me as a name. I have as many anonymous pieces as designer pieces on my stand.'

Domestic Totem –
'A fireplace from the
60s by the Belgian
manufacturer Don-Bar.
It's super rare and really
sculptural. I love pieces
that fall somewhere
between the utilitarian
and sculpture; I like
objects that are a little
out of the ordinary.'

The Secret Life of the Puces — 'Hassan and Hocine are porters. Porters have been an integral part of this micro-economy of the Puces since the beginning. Since I try to reconfigure my stand every week, this requires a lot of handling, so fortunately they are there to help manage the logistics, to transport, to wrap, to install; they are essential to the functioning of the Puces.'

Marchés placés sous vidéosurveillance
(Loi n°95-73 du 21/01/95 et décret n°96-926 du 17/10/96)

What is your expertise, speciality or particularity?
It was really an aesthetic shock when I discovered the design of the 60s and 70s. I love this period for its unbridled creativity and novel forms, and the notion of comfort too. It's a move away from the rigour of modernism towards more playful, more generous and organic forms. But I really function on impulse, I don't put any barriers in place, I can like a painting from the 90s or an armchair from the 40s. What excites me in this profession is finding rare pieces, pieces that are little seen or known that will amaze people, and that are hard to find. I much prefer to buy a piece I don't know, than to buy a classic that everyone knows.

Is there an image from the past that obsesses or inspires you?
The modern houses designed by the Bordeaux school on the Bay of Arcachon in the 60s and 70s unite my two passions: the design of that period and the Cap-Ferret peninsula, a place where I have many memories from childhood. This place was my first aesthetic experience, and gave rise to my love of design. I started out passionate about architecture but soon realized that architecture and design are very linked; designers are often architects and vice versa, and really, furniture design is just architecture on a smaller scale.

How did you get where you are?
After architecture studies in Bordeaux, I moved to Paris and landed a first internship at Artcurial auction house, in the design department. This is where I really discovered the world of collectible design, and the design of the 60s and 70s. I remember handling incredible pieces in the warehouses. After this internship, I did another one at the Galerie kreo which was very interesting because kreo presents a mix of both contemporary and vintage designer furniture. At the same time, I started buying and reselling. I started by going around to all the *brocantes* and *vide-greniers* in the Paris region, and I also started travelling — I would go back and forth to Belgium quite a bit, buying lots of things that I stored in the cellar of my building on Rue de Rennes and then resold on eBay. And after that a dealer from Serpette, now a dear friend, proposed that I help him run his stand. I accepted because it was a good opportunity and Serpette corresponded to my activity and my style. He gave me my start at the Puces.

Is there an element of magic to your work?
I think a lot about the decoration of my stand. It's always been very important. I find that the association of several rare pieces can create a kind of magic, can provoke very strong emotions, so I really take pleasure in the staging. I don't sell on online marketplaces, though I have an Instagram account, because for me, the pleasure of my job is in associating pieces with each other, and creating a dialogue. It's not just about buying objects and presenting them like a catalogue, it's really about creating decors. This has a commercial advantage too, because it allows clients to imagine things in a real-life environment.

Essential artisan or craft for you?
I have my pieces restored by quality craftsmen. The upholstery is a very important, very instinctive part of my business.

What has, or hasn't, changed at the Puces?
I would say that the Puces is professionalizing and moving upmarket. The stands, the displays and a younger generation are all participating in this revival. Because rents are now as expensive as those of a gallery space in Paris, dealers have realized that when they refine their displays and restore pieces, it allows them to better promote their merchandise. This is positive, it raises the bar. Today, to survive, you need business intelligence. Before, you just put something down and it sold. Today there is more competition, so to succeed you need business processes and commercial strategies.

How does the Puces relate to the larger antiques and second-hand market in Paris, and around the world?
It is one of the epicentres: there's the Puces, the auction houses and the galleries. At the international level, it is unrivalled.

What does *chiner* mean?
It's about scanning thousands of objects and finding the piece that will procure an emotion. The 60s and 70s are more fashionable now than when I started in 2012, so the pieces are harder and harder to find. You have to be present on all fronts, there really is no single rule. There are auctions, professional sales, the internet and Instagram, the network of second-hand dealers — more generalists than me who find pieces that correspond to what I am looking for — and the Puces itself, where I buy a lot. It's really the accumulation of all these sources that allows you to buy regularly.

Your best find?
A pair of brass andirons by Giacometti, an extraordinary find bought for a handful of euros early in my career.

What is unique about your practice?
I travel a lot to buy. It's a pleasure simply to travel, but it's also a pleasure because I find that we comprehend objects better when we see them in real life, when we see them in three dimensions. This is what provokes emotion.

What's your motto?
I really like this quote by Brancusi: 'Simplicity is complexity resolved.'

What is luxury?
To make a living from one's passion.

Aurélien Serre

Pop Icon – 'The Karelia armchair designed by Liisi Beckmann, and first produced by Zanotta in 1966. It almost looks like a toy, like a piece of Lego, and demonstrates in a very spirited and free way the experimentation with form so typical of the 60s. I had it re-upholstered in brown wool velvet. I really like brown because it has a very 70s side, but it remains a fairly natural colour. I really try to go towards natural colours, but when I use too many, after a while, I want to shake things up and use a bright colour.'

– 'An Italian floor lamp, "Tenaglia", by Francesco Buzzi Ceriani, 1969. This piece has a lot of style. Once again, it's super graphic, with its round and generous shape. It has quite a playful side too, with the globe that splits in half.'

Aurélien Serre

Wow Factor –
'The "Boomerang" desk by
Maurice Calka is an icon of the
6os, really legendary. A limited
edition, only around a hundred
pieces were ever produced;
it's super rare. This one comes
originally from a director's
office at Peugeot; a collector
sold it to me. It has these
really inflated, rounded organic
shapes, and its shininess is also
typical of that time. It's made of
lacquered fibreglass, and is in
perfect condition. Above hangs
a pair of Goffredo Reggiani
golden wall lights, and to the
right a "Helga" floor lamp by
Silvio Bilangione.'

Personal Collection – 'I have a passion for watches. This is my Audemars Piguet Royal Oak from 1972, designed by Gérald Genta. It's a legendary design that is quite emblematic of the 70s. I was lucky enough to buy it before it got really hot. Watches are like art, like antiques – the value fluctuates, depending on demand, the condition, the provenance, etc. Though there's an irrational side too. These worlds are all very connected because it's the same world of collectors, of aesthetes, of people who have an eye for detail and who love old things that reflect an era. Watches are a concentration of all that.'

Aurélien Serre

RAMDANE TOUHAMI

Artistic director, entrepreneur, hotelier
Art Recherche Industrie
www.a-r-i.ch

The Puces is where I started. 1992. Every weekend I came up from Montauban, where I lived in the countryside, to sell my T-shirts at the Marché Malik. It's the vibe of the Puces, I think, that I liked from the get-go. More the Puces than Paris actually, because it is after all my world. The Porte de Saint-Ouen part, where you have all the Blacks, the Arabs, the gypsies ... and the 'thieves' market. That's basically the Puces, it started like that, with the ragpickers, the guys who collect things from the trash and resell them. While the snobs don't want to go through that part, where you see people amassing all the filth from Paris and reselling it, and the guys who come looking for fake sneakers never go to Vernaison. You have many people going to the same place, but they don't cross paths. And that's something that always bothers me.

The city of Saint-Ouen is the most dangerous city in France. People don't know, but it's the place where the most people are killed. More than in Marseille. Every weekend, it's a grand bourgeois spectacle, alongside the poorest people, the illegal immigrants who sell what they find in the trash, alongside all the riff-raff of the suburbs. There is a fairly fascinating social division, it's capitalist fascism at its peak, it's a horrible and fantastic place at the same time.

I don't buy like everyone else. At the moment I'm building one of the largest collections in the world of independent newspapers from the gay, feminist, environmental, Black movements etc. I have the 1,100 Black Panther party newspapers, I bought them all. There is a profusion in the 1960s–70s of independent newspapers which is fascinating. Ninety per cent of the magazines we buy are not on the internet. Today everyone has the same image sources, but we want different sources. So it's very exciting, because it's going to annoy everyone, we're going to have information that others don't have. And we also have a bookstore in Paris, the Pharmacie des Âmes, where we're going to sell these things.

People think I'm obsessed with old things but I'm on the other side of the hill now. That is to say, I went from being a fan of old things to hating Mitteleuropa, all this old stuff, the nineteenth century. I think I missed out on 10 years of my life seeing what was new because I was a little too into old stuff. The world is moving forward but you're looking back.

Now I want to talk to people who think like me. I am an extremely left-wing guy, I am a guy open to the internationalist world, I campaign to pay more taxes, I give money to associations, I campaign for Palestine like no one else, I open schools, I do what I can. At the end of the day, you wake up and say to yourself, 'Shit, I'm no longer interested in working for these clients – I'm not against them, we've done great projects, but it is no longer my world. There are no people like me in these places.' So you say to yourself that you are going to use your expertise so that people like you can move forward too. At the Puces, in the white part, I'm all alone: buying furniture in Vernaison, at the Paul Bert Market and all of those places, guys like me, there's only me.

Ramdane Touhami photographed in the HQ of his creative agency, Art Recherche Industrie, in Paris

FRANÇOISE & ERWAN DE FLIGUÉ

Haute Couture – 'The three graces, wearing evening dresses. The one on the left is a silk chiffon by Maggy Rouff, circa 1938. Rouff was a very important fashion designer in the late 1930s and 40s, even if she was implicated, during the war, in the collaboration. The black one is from 1948, by the House of Worth, made from a very light rep fabric. The house was created in the 1850s by Charles Frederick Worth and is extremely important from a historical perspective, because Worth laid down the principles of haute couture. Though for me the best generation is not Charles Frederick, but the second generation, Jean-Philippe and Gaston, because Jean-Philippe had enormous talent; even Poiret hated him. And the third silhouette on the right is an anonymous white rayon dress, with a rayon damask evening coat.'

Françoise & Erwan de Fliqué

174

A Colour Revolution –
'This is a classic day dress, circa 1865, in jacquard wool, with a cotton lining. It was a solid, inexpensive, no-fuss dress; bourgeois, without being haute-bourgeoisie. The purple is a characteristic Aniline purple. Aniline is a chemical residue, generally obtained from the combustion of coal when we produced lighting gas. It was a disgusting, super-toxic residue which smelled very bad, and from this residue, a German chemist developed a whole range of chemical dyes, with very beautiful, very characteristic colours, which were terribly fashionable between the 1860s and 70s. The first was magenta. It's called magenta because it was launched around the time of the Battle of Magenta in 1859. These dyes came from petrochemicals and are quite characteristic of the second industrial revolution.'

Tell us about your profession.

E: We work the old-fashioned way, by sourcing individual pieces that we sell in the boutique. We never buy bundles of second-hand clothes from sorting factories, and rarely go to auctions. Because what amuses us is the thrill of the find. I don't buy to sell, I sell to buy ... Fortunately Françoise is more reasonable. We clean and restore everything ourselves, otherwise we would have to sell at much higher prices. We keep prices down to sell quickly, so that I can go back to hunting ...

Who are your customers?

E: Although the Puces is a tourist attraction, tourists are not really our clientele. They misunderstand what we sell. First, you have to gently explain to them that most old silks are too fragile to wear. And then, they are often obsessed with brands, while the custom-made dresses by anonymous dressmakers from the 30s to 60s are generally of a superior quality than contemporary designer ready-to-wear. Our real customers don't come to us by chance. They are often devotees of a specific era. Of course, we supply costume designers too, both for cinema and theatre. And we still see some fashion designers, although much less than twenty years ago. As for collectors, almost all of them are looking for the museum piece.

What are you most proud of?

F: A great satisfaction that our activity at the Puces provides us is to sometimes permit certain pieces to be found by the person for whom they were truly destined.

What has, or hasn't, changed at the Puces?

E: For years, right up until 2008–9, which roughly corresponds to the subprime crisis, fashion designers were responsible for 40 or 50 per cent of our turnover, which is colossal. They crowded in, looking for old pieces to copy. But times have completely changed since then. One more thing I hate about brands is that clients have become simply consumers, who buy a brand instead of buying a piece, and conscious of that, sales and marketing people have taken over fashion houses. The designers no longer really have any power. And this demonstrates that the whole system is sick.

Why the name?

E: It originates in a bad joke. Maurice de Saxe was a great French general who served under Louis XV. The French armies were largely shit under Louis XV, and most generals were bad, but he was the least bad. One day when he was on a mission in the provinces, he convinced a local seamstress that the ruffles fashionable women were starting to put at the bottom of their dresses were called *'falbalas'*. And the poor girl believed him. It's always very naughty to take advantage of the naivety of silly girls. But since there is a god for silly girls, it became true, it started a trend. And then it became a film by Jacques Becker, starring Raymond Rouleau. I like Becker and what's more, all the costumes in the film are by Marcel Rochas, who was a terrible collaborator during the war, but was not entirely lacking in talent. There are lowlifes who have no talent, like Chanel, and there are lowlifes with talent, like Rochas.

Your favourite designer, artisan or artist?

E: Vionnet, like everyone else, because Vionnet is one of the greats. I have always really liked Madame Grès, not only for the draping; very simple things that she did in seaside fashion are also a delight. And Jacques Fath, for the touch of fantasy in everything he did. But there are many designers from whose collections I like certain pieces; I can love them for very different reasons. For example, I love everything tailored at Schiaparelli, but the soft dressmaking is less good. For the soft dressmaking of the same period, I prefer Vionnet or Grès. Just as one can love Alaïa's dresses and Mugler's suits.

Your best find?

F: The magic of this profession led us to a fabulous trunk that had belonged to the great dancer and actress Ludmilla Tchérina. It had accompanied her on tour for several years, and contained magnificent costumes and personal mementos. Logically, these extraordinary contents should have been broken up, because very beautiful dresses by great designers would have particularly delighted bidders in the auction rooms. But to us it felt important to maintain this precious testament to history intact. We thought of one of our clients, a former choreographer passionate about Russian ballet, a great collector of vintage fashion and especially ballet costumes, who seemed to incarnate the perfect heir to such a unique treasure.

Your greatest extravagance?

E: I don't like talking about my style much, but generally what I wear dates from between 1880 and 1939, even if I have some stuff from the 40s. There are periods that I don't like. In menswear, the whole 50s and 60s is generally very annoying – the 50s is so boring for men, but I love it for women – though there are some amusing things in American fashion, but I don't want to dress in American clothes. So the only recent style I wear would be from the 70s, because there are some cuts that I find fun.

What's your motto?

E: I really like that principle of Brecht's, that things belong to whoever makes them better. I think that the pleasure I have in doing this work is a little of this order. When I go hunting for pieces, and I spot, on top of a pile of crap, an old piece that no one else has spotted, I feel like I've saved something, and that it will be of use to someone else. This is really important for me. In fact, it's political. I am someone who detests the entire consumer society. My furniture, most of my books, all my everyday objects, my clothes, almost everything I own is older than me, and I take care of it. And I would like most of the things that are older than me to survive me. It's not about objects that pass by and that I consume. I consider myself to be simply a custodian.

Françoise & Erwan de Fligué

176

Cultural Inheritance — Eugène Atget, *Chiffonnier*, c. 1900. 'At the Puces, everyone is their own boss, and they deal with other people as best they can. And ultimately this culture can be traced very far back, to the beginning of the Puces, to the time of the *chiffonniers*, the ragpickers. They too were independent people, who did not have to enter into a social hierarchy, with someone giving them orders. And there is still a bit of this anti-authoritarian attitude among certain dealers today, including me.'

Contemporary Couture – 'There are still some interesting, very talented designers today. For me, the most beautiful example is Iris Van Herpen, she has insane talent. She works with remarkable intelligence. Nothing is more beautiful than an Iris Van Herpen dress when it moves, when there is a body in it. It's absolutely magical. I had the luck to attend her first fashion show, in haute couture, when she arrived in Paris. It was the biggest revelation I've ever had at a show by far. Because she has developed many things technically, with modern means, to make something new and beautiful. She uses a 3D printer a lot. I don't at all romanticize historical things, what interests me is to return to pure creation as we did in the time of the Modernists. I don't like Postmodernism.'

Françoise & Erwan de Fligué

Potted History – 'This is a quality creation from the 40s by an anonymous French seamstress. We began to see more zips in the 1940s, but they had been around for a while at that point. The zipper existed from the beginning of the 20s, but no one knew quite what to do with it. There is a fairly famous example of a piece by Madeleine Panizon, who was the milliner who worked with Paul Poiret, who in 1925 made a hood with a zipper all the way down the back. It is very beautiful. There's one in the Palais Galliera. Dresses from the 1930s can look very strange sometimes, as there was a bit of a tendency – because zippers looked so modern – to show them off right at the front of the dress, rather than to hide them. I remember a Schiaparelli dress from 1934 or 35 with a huge diagonal plastic zipper down the front.'

Empire Dress – 'Under Napoleon (1804–15), dresses were made of sheer cotton chiffon, with a high waist just under the breasts. During this period, we stop focusing on the waistline to focus on the bust. Empire dresses were also completely see-through, and women no longer wore much underwear. We're starting to see a little bit of corsetry again, a "ninon" corset, which was just there to support the bust and distinguish the breasts into two separate globes. The chiffon is entirely embroidered in Point de Beauvais, white on white. The dress is very sober, very distinctive.'

Françoise & Erwan de Fligué

Dressing Up – 'When I was a little boy, I was frustrated not to have a doll. So here I am making up for lost time. I really love to play with dolls, especially life-size ones. As I don't really have the temperament of a Pygmalion, I don't dare to dress real women, but I can compensate for it with my dummies, and I love that.'

Trade Secret — Costume designer Anaïs Romand in her workshop in Romainville: 'Almost always when I have a project where I need vintage material, or which takes place in past eras, I will go and see all the dealers that I know at the Puces, quite a long time before I really even start working on it, to tell them that I'm going to work on such and such a century, an era, a milieu. In France, in cinema and theatre, the era most often portrayed is the nineteenth century. There's a considerable body of literature that is constantly adapted for cinema. What's good about Erwan and Françoise is that they themselves wear the clothes, so they know how the garments work on a body. And that's important, because I dress people too, I dress living people; I don't do research at the Puces to put pieces in museums.'

JEAN-PAUL JURQUET

Tell us about your profession.
With all antiques, all objects, it's the antique dealers who create them somehow, who bring them out of history, out of the attics, out of stagnation, and say 'Look at this.' They are artists … they are the ones who come up with the story. Maybe if I had never dismantled all the vaults in the Banque de France, they would have been scrapped, or abandoned. It's as if we exhume stories, put them before mankind. I've met people who have come up with incredible things, who have brought entire eras to light.

What is your expertise, speciality or particularity?
It's as if this profession is a forest and I wander off the path, from one side to the other. Today my theme is the Banque de France. It started gradually in 2006, but it is in a way a return, to childhood. I come from a family of scrap dealers who dismantle metal and recycle it. I evolved as an antique dealer towards objects that were a little more precious, a little more elaborate, then, one day, I'm offered scrap metal to dismantle, and I say yes, I know how to do that. And it's a new beginning. For me it's easy to dismantle banks; what was less easy at the beginning was that I dismantled and dismantled and everyone found everything very beautiful, but no one bought anything. At this point I identified with Bernard Palissy; I said to myself, soon I'm going to have to burn the furniture! Palissy invented a style of pottery, and struggled for years, until in the end he had nothing left, he could no longer even buy wood, so he burnt his furniture. And then, Eureka, he succeeded. So I said to myself, Jean-Paul, you are a Palissiste – and then my first customer arrived!

Is there an image from the past that obsesses or inspires you?
Sometimes when I'm in the banks to dismantle – it could be in the archive rooms, the vaults, or the basement – I imagine the guys who worked there, who built them, who arrived by train, by horse, and who did everything by hand. And when there was no natural light they used carbide lamps, which made smoke, and didn't really provide much light. They worked six days a week, perhaps twelve hours a day. Some of the things that we manoeuvre quite easily because we have very efficient machines are very heavy – they must have had their own techniques that were also very effective. The tools were hand tools. Everything was certainly extremely well prepared, numbered, pre-assembled in workshops, but still, the conditions were very, very different.

How did you get where you are?
My great-grandfather arrived from the Aveyron department and started in this salvage business. Scrap-dealing was a difficult job that others didn't want to do. It was ragpicking work. I remember when I was little, my aunts hanging rabbit skins out to dry in the garage. Back then, people who worked in scrap dealing wore a black coat, that you could even wear on Sunday over your white shirt. It was not a blue overall, but it placed you in a certain worker's class. I started in the business in the 1980s with antiques, because I knew a little bit about it. Because in my family, we did scrap metal, but also some antiques. I started doing that, I educated myself, I worked a lot. I started buying important things. I was focused on the eighteenth century, but I always had a line, a subject, a theme. Each piece has to tell a story, it has to be out of the ordinary. And along the way I also learned the bronzesmith trade and made a lot of things.

What inspires you?
I am also a collector, I have a few things … but maybe it's not me who tells their story, maybe they tell mine. Perhaps it's the object that brings out something in you, that changes your path. It's something that opens you up, like a fan. The whole horizon that lies ahead, and all the history that is there at the same time.

What has, or hasn't, changed at the Puces?
There are legends; it's said that once upon a time, more money was made in exports at the Puces than at Renault! But there are plenty of lies. It is a world of dreams and falsehoods too. There are plenty of fabulists. You meet them every week. And there have been seismic shifts in the business. For example, back in the day, people came from all over France, even from abroad, to sell here at Saint-Ouen. All the streets where you now see fake stuff, stuff from China, etc. was where, back then, people came to sell. And then one day, someone invented the professional antiques fair, in Montpellier, Béziers, Avignon, Le Mans, Chartres, etc. So those dealers don't come any more. Maybe tomorrow, people will buy second-hand, or maybe they won't. But what is certain is that in my day, you could invent yourself, everything was unscripted. It wasn't very difficult to make it up as you went along, whereas I think today it's harder, maybe because people don't operate in the same way – they need plans. We set off, like that, on an adventure.

What is the future of the Puces?
If I only knew! It's a bit like a film, or a play, it depends on the actors. I believe there are fewer dreamers today. But the Puces is also a reflection of society. The story of the Puces began with scrap dealing and has evolved. Today we are in a society based more on speculation than on anything else. The Puces is not simple, because it is about speculation in all directions, including real estate, with the price of rents always increasing. It changes the nature of the market.

Is there an element of magic to your work?
Some say it's magic, others say it's an illness. Once you catch it, you can't get rid of it. But there is a magic, the Puces is really effervescent. It's very powerful. Picture it, everybody comes here, everyone crosses paths. You find the guy who sells to survive, and the millionaires; the guy who comes to buy a pair of sneakers, and the incredibly erudite collector. And all the different nationalities. Find another place on the planet where that exists.

Jean-Paul Jurquet

Guiding Light – 'An exceptional bust of Victor Hugo, by a talented sculptor. It's a unique piece that I came across in the window of an antiques shop in a small town. I like seeing him there, with me. Sometimes I feel like he's looking at me. And sometimes I wonder if he's not thinking what I'm thinking. Sometimes he must say, "You're talking rubbish, Jean-Paul." For me, Victor Hugo is the greatest of writers. One of my favourite books is his last novel, *Ninety-Three*. He tells the story of the French Revolution, and asks, if the Revolution is just a guillotine, how can it work? I also like the fact that he was as capable of taking sides with one party as the other; not in order to say I am a royalist, I am a republican ... no, he saw good and bad equally everywhere.'

Status Symbol – 'The Banque de France loved these ornamental sphinxes, and presented them in the office of the director, on the desk, or mantelpiece, contributing to the aura of wealth and authority that reigned there. The model was originally designed by André-Antoine Ravrio an important sculptor in bronze, who had prestigious clients, including Napoleon. There was a fascination with ancient Egypt during this period, inspired by Napoleon's Egyptian campaign at the end of the eighteenth century.'

Jean-Paul Jurquet

Living History – 'We found these old shoes behind shelving in the Banque de France in Périgueux. The bank was built in 1878, so they probably date back to that time. I suppose they must have been worn out and forgotten. Espadrilles were the work shoes of the time; these are not a standard model, they are quite solid, with laces. I find them quite touching because they bring to mind the artisans who built the bank. The workers back then were very young lads, but they had a fine education, and drew beautifully. We often find, hidden behind shelving, drawings – usually of girls, poems – sweet things … they often signed their names.'

Latest Crush – 'I retrieved this key cabinet from a very small bank in Lens. I like it a lot. It's a nice size, and the only one I've seen that's red inside. This is a profession where you sometimes get attached to objects.'

Jean-Paul Jurquet

Image Bank — 'This is a photo I took in the archive room of the Banque de France in Périgueux, before we dismantled it. Lots of people don't understand where our pieces come from, they think they're new.'

Creative Refurb – 'I created this sideboard out of the top doors of steel shelving units recovered from the Banque de France, with their incredible "Camembert" or half-moon latches. I finished them with a slab of marble, old countertops that I recuperated years ago from a bank. Levanto marble is one of the most beautiful marbles that exists, there's a Levanto marble fireplace at Versailles for example. At some point I started inventing furniture models, I said to myself "Hold on, we can put that with that, and that with that." I like to combine different materials and elements from different banks and bring them back to life.'

Brand Identity – 'My stand is called the Salle des Coffres, so we need to have some *coffres* (safes). Commercially speaking, they don't work that well, but they're a powerful symbol of the bank.'

Bright Idea – 'These numbered aluminium bullion boxes were made to hold 4 x 12kg bars of gold, so 48 kilos of gold in each, for the national gold reserve. There were thousands of them. All buried underground, in a vault. Normally, these boxes are just melted down to make something new, but we present them here as decorative elements. Sometimes I buy things and I don't know what I'm going to do with them, and the idea comes later.'

Jean-Paul Jurquet

Maison James
Marché Vernaison
Alley 1, Stands 49–51

Furniture, paintings, objets d'art and sculpture from the seventeenth to the nineteenth centuries

DOMINIQUE JAMES

Classical Music – 'This pedal harp is quite a rare piece. It's Louis XVI period, late eighteenth century, by the famous French luthier Naderman. Musical instruments are very refined objects. Look at the beautifully carved crown in cherry, and the hand-painted soundboard. Naderman made Marie-Antoinette a harp as a present for her nineteenth birthday, and she became quite an accomplished player apparently.'

Still Ticking – 'In the eighteenth century, there was a clock in every room, on every mantelpiece. This is a quite rare, quite beautiful, pendulum clock from 1780, Louis XVI, which still works. Two superimposed circular wheels indicate the hour and the minutes. It's a very ingenious clock. The mechanisms in pendulums are normally vertical movements, however this mechanism functions with a horizontal movement, and all the cogs turn backwards, which is much more complicated.'

Dominique James

What is your expertise, speciality or particularity?
We specialize in eighteenth-century furniture. That's the core of our business. That's what I was educated in, what my uncle passed down to me. It's the century of Louis XIV, of Versailles, of the hall of mirrors … It's the Age of Enlightenment, the Lumières, this illumination of culture, a general radiance, which suddenly began to light up the world.

How did you get where you are?
Maison James began with my grandfather, during the war. He was born in 1896, and served in the First World War. Afterwards, my grandmother ran a restaurant on Rue Pasteur in Saint-Ouen, where she fed the railway workers, while my grandfather was a junk dealer who cleared houses, etc, with his cart. At first it was bed bases and mattresses, then he specialized in sewing machines, repairs and sales. My grandfather had two sons, my father and my uncle. My father set up at the Puces after the Second World War, in 1948, then in the 60s, after the Algerian war, my uncle joined him; before that they were at the Plaine Saint-Denis. They worked together and shared the responsibilities quite equitably: my uncle was more of a buyer and my father more of a seller. They were very complementary. And they raised the bar of the Maison James. In the beginning, Maison James was selling contemporary furniture, then my uncle launched into nineteenth-century furniture, then eighteenth-century furniture. At that time, eighteenth-century furniture was booming. There was a lot of it. This period was what we call the 'Trente Glorieuses', the period from 1970 to 2000, when business was really thriving. There was a huge export market, especially to the States, where French taste appealed greatly. This was when we bought up other stands at Vernaison and expanded.

You wouldn't be where you are without …?
My uncle went out seeking objects, he had a passion for it, and was able to communicate each piece's importance, to explain why it was interesting. One could say almost all objects are of interest, but there has been so much production in France, thousands and thousands of things, that you can drown in it. To really understand an object of interest, you need a certain amount of knowledge.

Is there an image from the past that obsesses or inspires you?
The dawn of what we now know as the Puces happened between the two wars, when poor people collected objects and furniture, and resold them here cheaply. I know people even today who are quite high up in the hierarchy of our profession, but who started out with a blanket on the ground of Rue Jules-Vallès, unpacking on Friday what they had found during the week. Sometimes they were lucky enough to find a somewhat rare piece which allowed them to establish themselves in a slightly more constructed way. It's hard to climb the ladder when you start on the ground, so it's very commendable when someone manages to do that.

What has, or hasn't, changed at the Puces?
The market has really thinned out, because of the internet, phones, social networks – it's very complicated. Everyone can see everything now, which doesn't benefit us. Before, we found our goods in places where there was no telephone, no television, no internet; it was just you and the object.

Have the internet and social networks changed the way you work?
The national library is more interesting than Google.

Tell us about your profession.
There is fierce competition between dealers, and always has been. The dealers mix, maintain civil relations, but they are nevertheless largely in competition, so there's little genuine camaraderie, few great friendships.

A good anecdote?
I was sent to an estate sale by my uncle and my father in the mid-80s at the Château de la Mercerie in Magnac-Lavalette following the death of the Réthoré brothers. It was one of the biggest sales I have ever attended. There was television, radio, local newspapers and all the dealers crammed into a tiny village. There weren't enough hotels to sleep everyone. The Réthoré brothers were pretty eccentric people, and their story is really fantastic. It was a lifelong dream for them to restore this castle – they were still building it in 1980, in debt up to their eyeballs. Unfortunately, they didn't have time to finish and the castle remained an unfinished work. They had grandiose ideas, inspired by the Palace of Versailles and others. They didn't have Colbert to save them from going broke though. They brought in Italian marble sculptors and had them sculpt all day long, statues of women, the four seasons in white Carrara marble, giant marble busts of Louis XIV, 1.5m high. There were enormous game presentation tables, that you only find in castles … Everything was of a scale that we're not used to. Huge.

Favourite time of day?
Our favourite moment is when there is a form of emotion, a form of excitement, and this often accompanies a purchase. Going to see an object in an auction is a moment where there is emotion. And even more so if you manage to acquire it.

Your best find?
A pair of life-sized statues of Roman warriors, seventeenth century, with their swords, their Roman helmets, in carved wood with their original polychromy intact. They were installed in Venetian palaces, between two rooms. I bought them in Marseille – we often went to Marseille with my uncle. He liked going there because he thought that because of the proximity to the coast, to Italy and all that, we found different things from Paris. A Louis XV chest of drawers was not of much interest to him. It bored him. He wanted more expressive things, he liked the spectacular.

Are you more tradition or revolution?
Tradition. If I was more revolution, I would have upended what I had been taught, innovated something different from my parents, but I have continued in the same vein.

Remembrance of Things Past – 'A beech wood bed, 1738, by Nicolas Blanchard, stamped with his mark. Blanchard was a famous cabinetmaker, in fact a *"chaisier"*, or chairmaker, which is a cabinetmaker who makes seating, and the bed was considered a seat. He worked under Louis XV. The most interesting thing about this bed is the quality of the carving, very pretty, and the curved bedstead. And the second particularity, quite exceptional, is that you could change the décor. This is the summer bed, but you could replace the wicker part with an upholstered frame in winter. Behind it, leaning against the wall on the right, is one panel from a huge painting that was in the Great Hall of the Château du Marais, a picnic scene, with the castle in the background.'

Living History – Erdal, gilder, at work in the Maison ARTE workshops. Located in the Marais since 1946, Maison ARTE specializes in the restoration of antique bronzes and the manufacture of decorative objects. 'The Faubourg Saint-Antoine hardly exists any more. The street is still there of course, but the community of artisans that occupied this neighbourhood for centuries is largely gone. On each side of the street, behind carriage entrances were gardens, workshops … everything necessary for the restoration, construction, and development of furniture. Cabinetmakers, varnishers, gilders, bronze artisans, marble artisans … all the crafts were grouped together. There are almost none left. When the little artists' studios with a glass roof and a small courtyard became worth 10,000 euros a square metre, it was soon over.'

For Sale – 'A pretty folding library ladder, late nineteenth century, oak. It's probably English, to judge from the screws. The woodwork is nicely done, the steps are hollowed out, and rounded, to make the ladder lighter, more practical, but at the same time it's very solid. Library ladders were in all bourgeois homes, particularly among the English, because in England there was always a room reserved for books: a library or a smoking room.'

Precious Gems — 'This little jewellery box is 300 years old, Louis XIV period. Not just anyone had a little box like this to store their jewellery. Its core structure is in pine wood, and it has little bronze feet. But what makes it rare is the marquetry, it has Boulle marquetry in tortoiseshell, brass, and pewter, with ebony fillets. The walnut interior is lovely too. And the little lock, how pretty it is. When we say Boulle, it references André-Charles Boulle, cabinetmaker to the king, in the Louis XIV, early Louis XV period, who invented the commode. His name has been popularized to describe objects featuring marquetry with a brass, pewter, or even a silver base. So we say Boulle furniture, or a Boulle decoration; we borrow his name because he perfected the technique.'

Stockpile – 'We've had this stockroom in the heart of the market for forty years, since my father and my uncle's era. There are objects here that have always been here, that have never been in the boutique: stock that never had its day in the sun. Many items are worthless, or at least, no longer have any value. There are periods which are finished, which will never come back in fashion: Henri II dining-room furniture, Restoration or Louis-Philippe period furniture. Our period – classical eighteenth-century antiques – is going down, while the 60s and the 70s are going up in value. Most of the pieces here arrived as part of box lots, one lot, two lots, three lots … things start piling up, accumulating, and then it gets out of control. There's stuff everywhere. It's quite impressive, isn't it?'

Le Grand Garcia

JACQUES GARCIA

Decorator
www.jacquesgarcia.com
www.chateauduchampdebataille.com

The Puces is a place where people from all walks of life come together, and I like that. I like mixtures, in general. It's a place where I immediately feel a collective festive spirit. If I spend a weekend in Paris, I go to the Puces.

My relationship to flea markets goes back to childhood. I had a father who was an intellectual, passionate about philosophy and music. And when I was 10 years old, we spent all our weekends at the Montreuil flea market. It was quite extraordinary. It was a place where you could find great things really for nothing. Unfortunately, Montreuil has become a place where only second-hand clothes are sold. My father was a very good *chineur*, especially passionate about books, which is why the Château du Champ de Bataille has a library of 20,000 volumes which, in large part, come from him. And he was lucky to have a kid who accompanied him, who had the same passion. That is to say, the idea of finding a masterpiece in a rubbish bin enthrals me. The Puces embodies the extraordinary idea of a child who is certain that he will enter a castle and find the Golden Fleece. For me that's what it's about.

I'm crazy about Androuet du Cerceau. I'm crazy about Le Vau. I'm crazy about Mansart. I'm crazy about Gabriel. I'm crazy about Ledoux. I'm crazy about Garnier. I'm crazy about Viollet-le-Duc. I'm crazy about Jean-Michel Frank. My variety of madness dates back 500 years, and it is these 500 years that forged me. This is how I got my education. We are lucky to live in a country where there is a masterpiece every metre and I strive to ensure that we don't put rubbish every other metre, so that the rubbish doesn't overtake the masterpieces one day. That's my obsession.

Jacques Garcia photographed in his office in Paris with his whippet, Livia.

Tombées du Camion, Peulan
Marché Vernaison
Allée 1, Stands 29 & 31
@tombeesducamion
and @peulan_paris

Vintage and forgotten lots, exclusive stocks from abandoned factories, mass-produced items, little sacred objects, artisanal treasures

CHARLES MAS

Personal Expression – 'To describe the scenography I create for the stands, I tend to repeat what other people say about it. People talk about mandalas, they talk about kaleidoscopes. A kaleidoscope is good, because it has a very childlike side. When you're a kid you can spend hours with a kaleidoscope, you move it a little and everything is magnificent, very shiny and bright. And what you see is incomprehensible and all that. But the scenography also has to do with my personality: it's really to do with my obsessive-compulsive side, hyper-organized, hyper-fanciful, super-rigorous. The profusion, the symmetry, the acrobatics, these are things that inspire me, that motivate me.'

What is your expertise, speciality or particularity?

My speciality consists of considering the object not for what it is, but for what it can become. The era, the material, the style are relegated to the rank of anecdote; the object is, for me, only raw material. I am one of the rare dealers to have so little applied knowledge in my field. I am an expert in my ignorance of the object for what it was. My particularity is to ignore its origin and only consider its destination.

Tell us about your stands.

Stand 29, Peulan: here hangs and rests a non-exhaustive inventory of lamp shades made in France between 1880 and 1980, chosen without any aesthetic or historical bias. The purchasing criteria are impulsive, instinctive but nevertheless demanding. The objective is to allow each of these lamps to combine with others to create or participate in a unique and surprising decor. Stand 31, Tombées du Camion: here you can find everything you didn't know you were looking for, organized in such a way that it's impossible to come across it other than by chance. It is a peremptorily poetic inventory of useless, senseless, unusable objects, except by those whose minds know how to adapt to the elusive fantasy of the absurd. But it is also, very prosaically, an invitation to buy with universal appeal.

Why the name?

Provocation, of course. I always wanted to tag *'brocanteur-voleur'* (second-hand dealer-thief) on the façade of my stand. To thumb my nose at the brocante world. So what if I tell you it fell off the back of a truck? People often ask me, where did you find this? And I say, well I can't remember, I was drunk. Let's not give too much value to objects. But to say something is worth nothing is quite a snub. It's also a reflection on property. One of the concepts of Tombées du Camion is that you can take what you want … I only sell small items that are typically put under lock and key, in a vitrine. This has been the logic of the second-hand dealer for centuries. Whereas I make everything accessible, which means you can steal, it's up to you. Those who have the means pay me for the objects, and those who don't, steal from me … Who cares, really. They're not museum pieces.

Who are you?

I am he who believes that life could have been boring, that fantasy is the most elegant of costumes, that vulgarity is a source of poetry, that humour is a matter of dignity, that money must be spent urgently, that objects are devoid of value and that wine spoils very quickly.

What inspires you?

Art brut, Dadaism, pataphysics and Madame Michu's doilies.

What is unique about your practice?

I have been trying for 15 years to convey a message that I strive to make abstruse. It's a life's work.

Tell us about your profession.

It's work that provides the opportunity to pass off neuroses as virtues, obsessions as stubbornness and compulsions as talent.

Why the Puces?

Because it is the most accessible playing field for an uncommon business and the place where it can best find its audience.

How do you explain your success?

I remember seeing the Godard film, *À bout de souffle*, on TV in the 80s, presented by Claude-Jean Philippe. It's the story of a guy, played by Belmondo, who kills a cop at the start of the film, and later he faces the camera, and says 'If you don't like the sea, if you don't like the mountains, if you don't like the city, go screw yourself!' It was far from being a sure thing that the film was going to be such a hit. Claude-Jean Philippe said something that made an impression on me. He said that the film happened at a moment when there was an unconscious need in the spectator to see that, and I think that Tombées du Camion is a bit like that; it was a case of right time, right place, I think.

Do you have to be a bit crazy to work at the Puces?

A bit is good, but it may not be enough.

Did you choose your market?

Rather it's the market that chose me. I've become very influenced by the trade of the Vernaison market, to the point of becoming a caricature of it. It has defined and shaped me. I am conclusively a seller of knick-knacks.

Your favourite tool?

Cash, it's the best medium for objects, along with cordiality.

What has, or hasn't, changed at the Puces?

Over the course of my professional life, the market has been completely revolutionized in terms of supply and demand. What used to sell no longer sells, those who bought are no longer customers, what sells today would never have sold before, and all these changes have attracted people that the Puces once rejected. The Puces has gone from a hub of the antiques market to a funfair straddling the worlds of decoration and entertainment. Despite this revolution, those who drive and energize this market remain generally uncommon types and collectively represent a nonconformist community and way of life.

How does the Puces relate to the larger antiques and second-hand market in Paris, and around the world?

It seems to me that the antiques and second-hand market probably revolves around the Puces, which functions as the backbone of this world. Trends are born at the Saint-Ouen flea market and end their lives at peripheral markets.

Is there an element of magic to your work?

Yes, we deliver marvels from oblivion, and by the simple act of buying them we bring them back to life, or perhaps to life.

A good anecdote?

One evening, it was raining heavily when Les Puces closed, and hoping that the rain would soon stop, I shared a few drinks with some neighbours. The weather refusing to calm, I resigned myself to returning to the Rue des Rosiers; after covering my head with my leather Perfecto jacket, I spy, about to jump into a taxi, the actor Vincent Lindon! Soaked and staggering a little, wrong-headed, and a little jealous of the aura of this good man, I bellow: 'Lindon, *dindon!* Shame … At first surprised, then intrigued, then angry, he pops his head out, and jutting out his chin defiantly, he snaps: 'Mas, *limace!*'

If you weren't at the Puces, where would you be?

At the bar.

Charles Mas

Business Model – 'Peulan is a collaboration with my wife Pauline d'Arfeuille. At Peulan, we create light installations – no one else is really doing this. I don't really know what people are looking for in lighting today, because we buy things that aren't necessarily in fashion and then combine them to our taste. It is also a question of margins and positioning: if I buy things that are in fashion, I will pay too much for them, so I won't make my margins, and I need to make high margins for my business.'

Puces Picnic — From left to right: Charles, Marie, Thomas, Nicolas, Sofía and Pauline. 'I work without external partners — all my business needs are taken care of internally. I have always had a great team, and having lunch together really helps bring us together.'

Key Material – 'You can't do much better than a white globe. It's timeless. It's a bit like the original light source, the sun, the moon … In lighting, everything kind of originates from the light bulb, which is an incandescent globe. We create dynamic installations, and a luminous globe has the advantage of better defining a curve, it creates points, and by using different sized globes, you can really create a sense of motion.'

218

Creative Freedom – 'Take an eye, associate it with anything and you have a person, you have a face. Stick an eye on anything, and that's it, it's alive. There's a slightly creepy side to it that I like too ... To begin with it was dolls' eyes that interested me, then one day I came across a stock of glass eyes for the war wounded. If I found tigers eyes, that would please me too ... You have varying degrees of freedom when you sell useful things, like chairs or tables, because you are facing a specific demand, but when you sell useless things like art, curiosities, things that are not functional, suddenly you can really express your taste.'

A NOTRE NIÈCE
A NOTRE MAMAN
A NOTRE CAM
LE CLUB DU 3ème AGE
A NOTRE
A MON F
FRÈRE
REGRETTEE
A MA S
A MON FILLEUL
A. NOTRE FILLE
MON CAMARA
GUES
MARADE
A MON FIANCE
A MON EPOUX

Charles Mas

Tastemaker — 'It's crazy when you realize that these epitaphs are not custom-made things, that there is a whole catalogue of them. It's fascinating to see everything that is already ready to go: "To the president of the association", "For our work colleague", "For my beloved aunt" … What can be annoying about the second-hand trade is the supply and demand element, which is not really linked to the taste of each person, to a dealer's sensibility. It's just "Ah well no, this thing isn't worth any money you see." It has no value because it's not rare, and rarity is tied to quantity. So, I only sell things in quantity, in multiples. It's very pretentious I know, but I see myself as a gallerist, who will say "I took on three artists in France, and I'm going to raise their value, because that's my taste." This is what I try to do with my objects.'

Junk Art – 'Provocation and obscenity interest me, are part of who I am. Few people run away screaming because I have vintage porn posters in my catalogue. They make people laugh in fact. You can't leave vulgarity only to vulgar people. Often as dealers we censor ourselves, try to blend in, and not rustle any feathers, but I am a dealer-artist … artist-dealer, it's a bit the same … It's a somewhat strange, unexpected marriage, but there have also been worker-priests. It's true that it's difficult to define yourself as an artist when you're a dealer; sometimes I'm comfortable with it and stand by it, and sometimes I'm ashamed to say it, especially in front of other dealers.'

DAMIEN VANNIEN-WENHOVE

Best Find – 'My best find so far is this painting, oil on canvas board, dated 1921 and bearing the monogram of the German artist Hans Christiansen. It took me a few years to identify the artist. This painting represents years of research and my first good purchase as a dealer. It's an Expressionist portrait close to the style of Van Dongen. It's really one of my favourite paintings. It would have appeared really new at the time, even shocking. The Post-Impressionist period was a period of experimentation, a sort of painting laboratory, which gave rise to the emergence of Modern art.'

Tell us about your stand.

It's the first stand when you enter the Marché Vernaison, a small space but ideally located. A family affair since 2009. Initially a generalist, I quickly specialized in painting, a true passion, essentially selling works from the end of the nineteenth century until the Second World War. This includes the late Romantic, Impressionist and Post-Impressionist periods, but also Expressionism and Modern avant-garde movements.

Your favourite period, movement, or style?

I love the Nabis and the Pont-Aven School, and also the Symbolist movement. It's hard to choose just one! The Nabi period is perhaps my favourite. It was quite revolutionary at the time. When we talk about the Nabis, we talk about Synthetism, which is to say how to provoke emotion through an image which is not a perfect academic rendering. It's about suggestion, with colour that induces feeling. It's a movement that is linked to the Pont-Aven School, a group of painters around Gauguin and Émile Bernard who painted many landscapes in Brittany with light that changed all day long. This gave an extraordinary range of possibilities.

An unforgettable piece or sale?

A fairly important Art Brut painting by a painter called Augustin Lesage that I bought in a consignment store. It's unforgettable in the sense that it was the first painting that I sold for a good profit. I can't say that it's a painting I particularly appreciate, but still I found it interesting. In our profession, we must always dissociate quality from our personal taste.

How did you get where you are?

My father trained as a carpenter and cabinetmaker, he restored furniture from the 40s, Ruhlmann, Art Deco ... so when you see beautiful things in your father's workshop it obviously sensitizes you to art. But I think there's an innate element, that I have a sensitivity to paintings, just as I could have had a sensitivity to cooking or something else. After that it requires work, and since I didn't study art history, it means a lot of books, a lot of trips to the museum, many auction rooms too. I used to go to auction rooms just to see the sales results, the prices, the items sold, without buying anything. There is an expression in our profession, we say '*faire son œil*', which is to say that you have to develop your eye so that it is used to seeing beautiful things. A dealer once explained to me that when I acquired a beautiful painting, I should keep it at home for a bit, make it my own, so that the eye becomes accustomed to the quality, which is how we get there in the end.

What makes a good dealer?

A sensitivity to art and a lot of knowledge. A certain sense of business too! Knowledge is the very essence of our profession in the sense that it allows us to make a decision to sell because we know what we are selling, so we are not afraid of losing money. And that also allows us to buy, as a good dealer is someone who buys at the right price. Knowledge is what makes the difference.

A lucky charm?

No, but I feel lucky on the 17th! I was born on 17/07/1987.

What is unique about your practice?

Dealers have a special relationship with objects, we are sensitive to an object's substance, to its history. Not everyone has this sensitivity, but from the moment you have it, it creates a world where you feel emotions towards things. Often with my daughters, or with friends, we play a game where we ask ourselves if we gained a superpower tomorrow, what would it be? Wouldn't it be funny to hold an object and be able to communicate with it, to know what happened, what it saw, who it had met?

Do you have to be a bit crazy to work at the Puces?

A part of me is also a collector, I like to own paintings. In our profession, there is something really of the nature of mental illness in needing to own a particular thing.

A piece of wisdom?

One of the first pieces of advice that one of my father's friends gave me when I started out was something very simple, which is that you don't buy for yourself, you buy to resell. Which means that we must never forget that what we do is a business. But of course I hold on to many pieces. Some I know exactly what they are and I just like them, and others I keep because I don't want to do the stupid thing of selling something for 1,000 euros, when in fact it's worth 30 or 40 thousand. But you also have to know how to sell, how to let go, because I know dealers who are so afraid of making a mistake they never sell anything, and so never actually have the money to buy other things. You have to find a balance.

What has, or hasn't, changed at the Puces?

Today the profession has become more difficult. That is to say, the market has thinned out a bit; you no longer find beautiful objects so easily. So when you have good ones, it's good to hold on to them a bit and make sure you get the best return.

An emblematic character from the Puces?

The singers from Chez Louisette, a guinguette-style restaurant unfortunately closed since Covid, but I hear that it might reopen. Located inside Vernaison, it was really a place apart, quite typical of the Puces, an historic guinguette, a little raucous, but impossibly charming.

Favourite place to eat or have a drink?

La Chope des Puces, a cult place for jazz manouche with a very special atmosphere. It's part of the magic of the Puces too, and contributes to the market's identity.

What are you most proud of?

To have become an independent dealer and to have overcome all the difficulties encountered.

Damien Vannienwenhove

For Sale – 'A drawing on paper dated 1894. The subject is really lovely and quite rare. The golf caddie or golf player from the nineteenth century are subjects which are not easy to find. That's what attracted me. It's not necessarily about a desire to find a very well-known artist, even if the picture is very well executed and there's a trace of a signature, it's really about the subject, which is so singular and charming.'

The Secret Life of the Puces – Rosélyne Raitiere, painting restorer. 'It's difficult to find a restorer who suits you. Restoration, especially of a painting, isn't an exact science. It's a matter of instinct and personality, but it's also pure business, because when you have a painting that cost 100 euros that you sell for 400, you can't put 200 euros into restoration. It's about price and skill and personality too. Now that I know Rosélyne my restorer well, when buying, I know what can or cannot be restored. But there are paintings where you cannot know in advance if by having it restored it will lose its charm. Even just a simple cleaning can completely transform a painting. And sometimes you even discover a signature – it's happened to me a few times – which allows you to identify the painter.'

Damien Vannienwenhove

Damien Vannienwenhove

Artist Unknown – 'Provençal school, oil on panel, from the late nineteenth century, in the middle of the Impressionist period. No signature, but some inscriptions on the back that I haven't had time to research yet. It's a painting that is more traditional than I would typically buy. But I like the landscape with these two characters in the middle like that, we wonder what they are doing; there is a quite calming, quite interesting atmosphere. I think it's a scene of fishermen having a little picnic. On the left are ruins, a kind of fort, to the right on the small hill I think it's a fishermen's hut, with the town in the background. I like the composition, with these characters in the centre of the painting which attract the eye even though they are very small and almost blend into the landscape. It appears to be a landscape of the South of France. I'm curious to know where it is – it's true that the moment you manage to discover the location of a painting, you can sometimes then determine the artist.'

School of Life – 'I've spent a lot of time at the Musée d'Orsay, developing my eye and giving myself a sort of self-taught apprenticeship. It's a place I go regularly because the collections are crazy, with so many paintings from the nineteenth century, paintings by Corot … there's a room on the Nabis with Vuillard and Bonnard and Vallotton, on the Pont-Aven School, on Gauguin, there's a room with a few Symbolists; on the top floor is a room dedicated to Impressionism which is extraordinary, which features Caillebotte's *Les Raboteurs*, and has a fantastic view over Paris when you peer through the clock face. It's an important place for me. I also went to the library a lot, a research library with archives and many *catalogues raisonnés*, many books and documents that cannot be found elsewhere.'

Ongoing Research – 'Oil on canvas, nineteenth century, there is a trace of a signature on the bottom right. The subject is extraordinary because fire scenes are rarely depicted, which is what initially motivated my purchase. It gives a really special atmosphere, a very special play of light, a sort of chiaroscuro; and then there is the historical aspect. In this instance, we can see from how the frame is mounted that it appears to be a French chassis. So I'm leaning more towards a Parisian scene. I am carrying out research because I would like to know what fire it is. Is it the Faubourg Saint-Antoine, or the Bazar de la Charité in 1897? There were not that many big fires in Paris in the nineteenth century, early twentieth. I've tried to identify the uniforms of the firemen. I'm still researching.'

Family Affair – 'My father Philippe is a dealer, he used to come to the Puces on Friday mornings with his finds of the week and sell to dealers here. Then he was encouraged to open his own stand, and I joined him soon after. Today my father is more of an artist than a second-hand dealer, he has made many things in metal, wooden sculptures, and then he really came into his own with sculpture in plaster. He makes totems, masks, a bit in the spirit of Cocteau, but he really has his own style. He works under the pseudonym Philippe Valentin. You can google him.'

Damien Vannienwenhove

Rabbit Hole — 'Pointillist school, oil on canvas, early twentieth century. Pointillism is a Post-Impressionist movement; Impressionism lasted quite a long time, but Pointillism was really a little capsule in time, which is why we don't find that many paintings, which gives them a particular interest. It's unsigned, and when we look at it closely, we sense that perhaps the painting is not quite finished. So that adds a bit of mystery. And I find the painting's panorama format brilliant, and all the symbolism of the two women posed like that. It makes me think of a painter called Théo van Rysselberghe. And I was wondering what the village could be behind and perhaps it's Saint-Paul-de-Vence, in Provence, a place where there were quite a few Pointillist painters. It's one of those paintings that I decided to keep and research. I don't want to sell this painting today and then in five years open the *Gazette Drouot* and see it there. It's usually a bit of an investigation when you buy a painting, there are clues that put you on the alert, you say to yourself, hey, it could be this or that painter; it's like a treasure hunt.'

JLF Antiquités
Marché Biron
Alleé 1, Stands 39, 40 & 41
and L'Usine, showroom 27
@jeanluc_ferrand
www.jeanlucferrand.com

Antiques and objets d'art, from the
eighteenth century to contemporary

JEAN-LUC FERRAND

Rarity – 'A small nineteenth-century two-seater Transition-style sofa in moulded and gilded wood resting on four tapered and fluted legs. It is a model which is quite rare, because it is heavily sculpted, both on the backrest and on the front crossbars, and the feet. It has a lot of charm, is very decorative, a little more opulent than usual, with lovely proportions. The tripartite back like this, with the medallion in the middle, is unusual. We had it re-upholstered in a blue, Louis-XVI-style fabric, with a motif of medallions, laurel wreaths and flowers.'

Jean-Luc Ferrand

What makes the Puces unique?

It took an incredible conjunction of circumstances to bring forth this village that we now call the Puces. This place is not the result of a developer or some visionary saying at some point: 'Hey, I'm going to make the biggest antiques market in the world, here in Saint-Ouen!' No, this place was born from a combination of natural circumstances, it was an evolution. From multiple political, human, social and cultural factors and interactions. What if the prefect of Paris had not evacuated the *biffins* from Paris? What if the Parisian tradition of the weekend stroll beyond the city limits had not existed? What if the duty on goods entering Paris had not existed? What if the demilitarized zone around the old ramparts of Paris where the first *biffins* were placed had not existed? What if, if and if … Would the Puces have seen the light of day? Probably not. This is what makes the Puces unique, unrivalled and impossible to reproduce. It does not reflect the vision of a person, but of life, with its meandering, its interactions, its movements.

What has, or hasn't, changed at the Puces?

The Puces has adapted to change. With the internet and the opening up to competition, dealers have had to professionalize. To remain competitive in the face of the growing supply of antiques online, dealers have been forced to develop their skills, their knowledge, but also improve services and what is now called 'customer experience'. We must attract the customer and offer a unique and pleasant buying experience. What has not changed: the very structure of the Puces, its organization into diverse and varied markets each with its own personality; the eclectic nature of its visitors; the huge variety on offer.

Does the Puces make the world a better place?

What's important to me is to contribute to bringing harmony to people's homes. It's quite nice to provide environments that are revitalizing, objects that give pleasure to people, that people enjoy having at home. That's important, we need that, especially today — we all have to get up, go to work, make money … If you can come home and it's decorated with things that you like, which make you feel better. That's my modest contribution.

Tell us about your profession.

This business is also a matter of perspective, of taste, of sensibility, and in the end you need to express the very personal taste you have for things, to express who you are.

What is your expertise, speciality or particularity?

We mix quite a bit between classic and modern. I think it's a shame to concentrate on this or that period, and by necessity, exclude others. I find that every era has very pretty things, had very good craftsmen, great savoir-faire. What interests me is to *chiner*, to go hunting for pieces which I find decorative, which I find interesting, aesthetically, also sometimes for technical reasons. I don't have the nature for being hyper-specialized in an era, it soon bores me, but that's my own temperament. I totally understand people who go deep into an area, who know it inside out, and with that expertise enrich those who buy the pieces.

What inspires you?

It seems obvious now to make a chair that stands on four legs, but it took a while to get there. We evolved from medieval things, very heavy, practically untransportable, things. Small chests with a seat on top. Then, little by little, as techniques developed, cabinetmakers made increasingly lighter seats. Until the eighteenth, nineteenth centuries, chairs were made of wood, and then in the twentieth, we started to use materials derived from petrol, plastic, which gave rise to new forms … All this is part of the continuum of the history of furniture, which uses new technologies, sometimes invented for completely different reasons, but which designers reappropriate to make furniture of their time. Now we make chairs with 3D printers. We've gone from the chest to the 3D printer, and that's interesting.

Is there an image from the past that obsesses or inspires you?

It was enough for Marie Antoinette, for example, to receive a new type of chair, or other piece of furniture, for the people who courted her to try to buy the same thing; there really was a phenomenon of mimicry, because you had to belong to a certain circle. The king or the queen or the people close to them, people like Madame de Sevigny for example, who were renowned for their taste, were a bit like the influencers of their day. There were people who did this out of snobbery, but there was also real intellectual curiosity, for example for foreign culture, for Japan, for China. Objects were admired, copied, and reinterpreted by French artisans.

What is unique about your practice?

I've developed this profession as a proper business which is rare, because ultimately it's a fairly individualistic job, because people often distrust each other, and don't like to share their knowledge or their network. That's not my mentality. I like to work in a team.

What are you most proud of?

To have succeeded in developing my business while maintaining a certain morality, certain ethics, that's important to me. We're not obliged to give in to all temptations. It's a milieu where money is at stake, where there are temptations to behave badly to gain money. I think there is no point in behaving like that, because anyway, you reap what you sow. I prefer to develop healthy relationships. I have always based my success on that, both with customers and with suppliers, and today I reap the rewards; people trust me.

Why the Puces?

Son of an antique dealer and an architect, I have been immersed in this milieu from a very early age, and it appealed to me right from the start. It's a total shambles, a world full of life, surprises, dreams … A quite magical world, just like life itself, and us humans.

Jean-Luc Ferrand

Political Statement – Guillaume Legouge of the JLF team installing the inflatable sculpture 'Nana' by Niki de Saint Phalle for Flammarion, signed, 1996. Niki de Saint Phalle began making her inflatable Nana sculptures in 1968, in an effort to democratize her art. 'It is a decorative object, it is rather nice, but with no veritable value as an antique.'

Family Affair — 'My daughter, Victoire. I'm happy that one of my daughters wants perhaps to join me, to work in the same profession. I did not push any of my children to do this job, because I really wanted it to come from them. My mother helped me a lot, saved me a lot of time, by explaining how this world works to me, its codes. It's easier when your parents are in the trade, because from the start you are surrounded by conversations around art, around painting, around furniture, around beauty.'

UE DES ROSIE

Jean-Luc Ferrand

Living Traditions – 'Pierre Chapo, a French architect and designer from the post-war period, was very creative, inventing new forms, while also trying to rationalize manufacturing processes. His contemporaries in French avant-garde, such as Pierre Guariche or Pierre Paulin explored new materials, like plywood, or metal, but Chapo maintained an attachment to French woodworking traditions. Here we see the T14A Pillar Elm wood table, circa 1960. Chapo said: "The design of our table T14 conveys the weight, strength and texture of solid wood better than any other." And one of the most sculptural creations in the Chapo catalogue, the S45 chair from 1979 is made using a patented wood-joining technique Chapo developed and called the "Chlacc" system (Construction Homogène Lamellée Assemblée Collée Cloué, or Homogenous Laminated Assembled Glued Nailed Construction).'

Jean-Luc Ferrand

The Secret Life of the Puces — Fabien Schmidt, cabinetmaker, in charge of the restoration workshop: 'At JLF, I take care of everything to do with the restoration and repair of the objects we sell. It's very gratifying and fulfilling to breathe new life into something that has been forgotten, lost, damaged, worn out; to give it new life and give it back its original lustre. I am a trained cabinetmaker, but through my work I have to handle many other materials and techniques: marble, or the electrification of a lamp or a chandelier. I do lacquer, traditional Japanese lacquer, gilding ... Out of necessity, I do a little bit of everything.'

Trade Secret — In the window of hardware shop Dugay. Fabien Schmidt: 'Dugay is my main supplier. They've been at the Puces forever, I knew their parents. They are important partners connecting us with the manufacturers and supplying us with all the professional tools and products we need, and finding us out-of-the-box solutions too. There are more and more artisans and workshops at the Puces, which is a like a hub revolving around art and antiquities where many different professions assemble and mingle.'

Scandi Style – 'Two-seater teak and leather sofa by Swedish designer Arne Norell, 1970s. It's quite clever how the leather cushion is delicately moulded over the wooden structure, a bit like you see with Brazilian furniture. It's very comfortable, you're not lost in a big sofa with lots of fabric, but you are very well supported. Typical of Danish design, it's both sober and elegant.'

Landmark – 'I often have lunch at La Péricole. Dany, the owner, has been here since 1999. The café is at the heart of the Puces, next to the L'Usine and Jules-Vallès markets. These markets, as well as the streets Rue Jules Vallès and Rue Paul-Bert, are particularly active on Thursdays and Fridays, and focused on sales between dealers, professionals. A lot of *chineurs* meet at the Péricole in the morning to have coffee, to discuss what they have bought, what they have seen. It's where people meet to do business too. Everyone knows each other there.'

Jean-Luc Ferrand

A Chronology of Antique French Furniture Periods

Medieval
1300–1500
|
French Renaissance
1500–1589
|
Louis XIII
1589–1661
|
Louis XIV
1661–1700
|
Régence
1700–1730
|
Louis XV (Rococo)
1730–1760
|
Transition
1760–1774
|
Louis XVI
1774–1785
|
Directoire
1785–1799
|
Empire
1804–1815
|
French Restoration
1815–1830
|
Louis-Philippe
1830–1850
|
Second Empire / Napoleon III
1850–1890
|
Modern Style and Art Nouveau
1880–1925
|
Art Deco
1920–1939

Acknowledgements

This book has been a thrilling rabbit hole down which I am still falling. Thanks to all the dealers and everybody else who guided my adventures. A special shout-out to Margaux Delprat and Elsa Dubois (Paul Bert Serpette), Medhy Allaouchiche Gerault (Biron), and Béatrice Mellet and Edith Lory (Dauphine) for their assistance.

Thanks to Andrew Hansen, Rochelle Roberts, Francine Brody, and the whole team at Prestel. Bravo for making such bold and inspiring books.

Thanks to Alexandra Marshall for whipping the introduction into shape, and to Flora Natasha Temple for production assistance.

Thanks to Gilles Tombeur for his steadfast encouragement and another brilliant idea. Thanks dear Lee.

Thanks to Bertrand Belin for the songs.

The Paris Flea Market is part of my ongoing Mkrs. project, conjuring spirit of place by identifying living networks and mapping creative DNA.

Follow us on Instagram
@mkrs.family

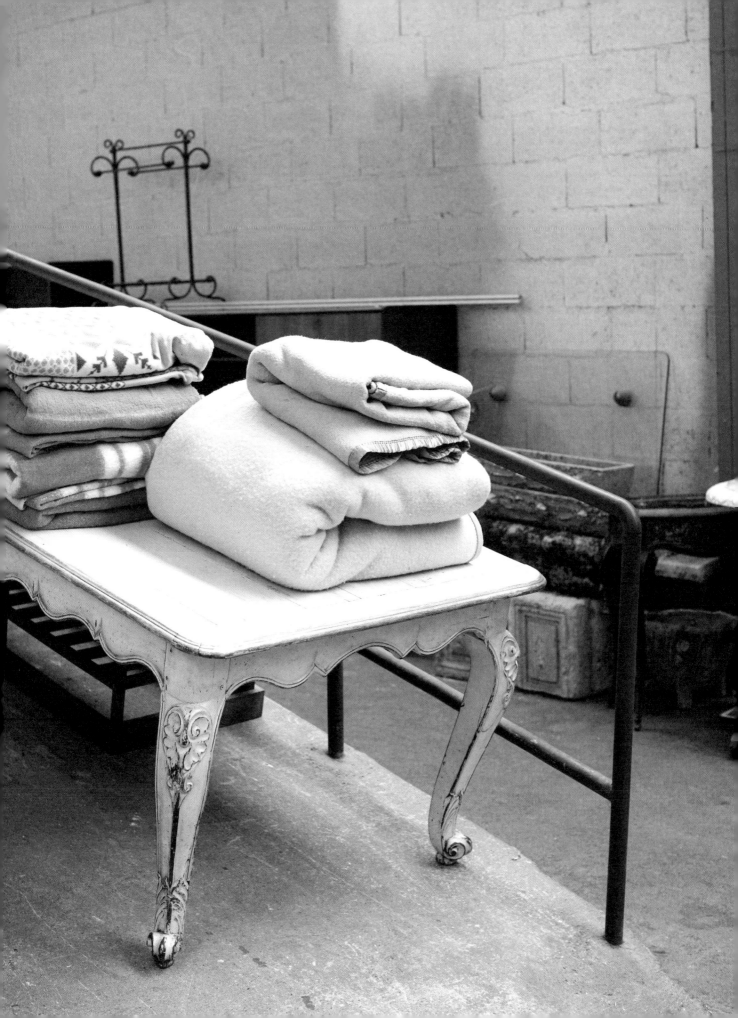

un tiroir dépareillé
une pelote de ficelle deux épingles de sûreté un
    monsieur âgé
une Victoire de Samothrace un comptable deux aides-
    comptables un homme du monde deux chirurgiens
    trois végétariens
un cannibale
une expédition coloniale un cheval entier une demi-pinte
    de bon sang une mouche tsé-tsé
un homard à l'américaine un jardin à la française
deux pommes à l'anglaise
un face-à-main un valet de pied un orphelin un poumon
    d'acier
un jour de gloire
une semaine de bonté
un mois de Marie
une année terrible
une minute de silence
une seconde d'inattention
et . . .

cinq ou six ratons laveurs

un petit garçon qui entre à l'école en pleurant
un petit garçon qui sort de l'école en riant
une fourmi
deux pierres à briquet
dix-sept éléphants un juge d'instruction en vacances
    assis sur un pliant
un paysage avec beaucoup d'herbe verte dedans
une vache
un taureau
deux belles amours trois grandes orgues un veau marengo
un soleil d'Austerlitz
un siphon d'eau de Seltz